PERFECT PHRASES™

for

FUNDRAISING

PERFECT PHRASES™

for

FUNDRAISING

**Hundreds of Ready-to-Use Phrases
for Appealing to Donors and Getting
the Funding You Need**

Dr. Beverly Browning

New York   Chicago   San Francisco   Lisbon   London   Madrid   Mexico City
Milan   New Delhi   San Juan   Seoul   Singapore   Sydney   Toronto

1 2 3 4 5 6 7 8 9 10   QFR/QFR   1 8 7 6 5 4 3 2

ISBN   978-0-07-179373-5
MHID   0-07-179373-9

e-ISBN   978-0-07-179374-2
e-MHID   0-07-179374-7

Contents

PART I

PERFECT PHRASES FOR FUNDRAISING LETTER CAMPAIGNS

CHAPTER 1

The Order of Information for Reader Impact

This first chapter is essential to your success in raising funds to meet your organization's financial needs and gives you a glimpse of the myriad perfect phrases that I'll introduce in Part One: Perfect Phrases for Fundraising Letter Campaigns. Recipients of standard fundraising letters are bored and tired of reading unordered, random appeal paragraphs. They expect to see *who* needs their money rather than what organization needs their money. Putting the right phrases first and in impacting order can make the difference in having your funding appeal read or tossed. Approximately 95 percent of electronic and hard mail appeals are reader turnoffs. So, what's in the 5 percent of these types of appeals that make the funding cut? Why do readers want to read more and pull out their checkbooks? In this chapter, I will show you how to use words and the order of the words in perfect phrases to play on the hearts and wallets of potential donors. The most common *old standby* formats for reader impact are:

- electronic fundraising appeals (sent via e-mail)
- postal mail fundraising appeals (sent via the U.S. Postal Service)

Once you understand the psychology of funding appeal readers, you'll know how to capture their attention with words. Let's look at the basics of what impacts a reader's psyche.

Personalization Impact. Potential contributors want to believe that the letter or e-mail was written only to them and just for them. This means you must be on target when it comes incorporating the reader's name, title, organization's name, and a common shared value (shown in the person's contribution history priorities) into your electronic and/or postal mail appeals.

How can you increase your chances of impacting a funding appeal reader? You can gain an edge by thoroughly researching each and every recipient of your funding appeal. Use your favorite Internet search engine to locate critical information on each member and/or organization in your target audience for the appeal. Call potential donors' business offices to double-check the correct way to address them (Mr., Miss, Ms, Dr., Rev., or Honorable). Ask for the correct spelling of their first and last names. Also, ask if they prefer to use a nickname.

For example, William may prefer to be addressed in correspondence as Bill or Billy or Willy. To use William means that you know nothing about the reader and that you did not take the time to find out how to capture the reader's attention in the first line of your letter! Madeleine may prefer to be addressed as Ms. Jackson; to use Maddie could be a reader turnoff.

Giving Priorities Impact. Potential contributors most often give to causes or organizations that have a familiar place in their lives or corporations or foundations. By this I mean, for example, if Harry Jones, the CEO of Wondercast (a medical supplier of body cast wraps) who has traditionally contributed to orthopedic-related causes, receives an appeal for sponsoring a 5K marathon to raise money for asthma education, it's not going to impact Harry at all unless he or someone close to him suffers from asthma.

Outline for Electronic Fundraising Appeals

Using e-mail to solicit funds is not as easy as it appears. First, if your e-mail address is not in the reader's electronic address book, your e-mail will likely be routed away from the in-box to the trash, spam, or junk mail folder. Remember, the most important reason for using e-mail to raise funds is to drive the readers to your organization's website where they will be able to read more about the organization's background and history, mission, board members and affiliations, and programs and activities. Your e-mail is the introductory tickler (bait) to get them to click through to read more details. Once the readers are on your website, they will see the link for making a contribution. And if you're smart, giving won't be a five-web-page event, but a smooth and easy click, enter information, and submit!

Let's get started looking at the most important components in what will become your award-winning e-mail to potential contributors.

1. Subject Line. The subject line in any e-mail is the magnet for getting the reader to open the message. This means that the subject line must appeal to the reader's sense of duty or responsibility. You have two options for the types of subject lines that engage an e-mail recipient to actually open the e-mail and read its content. Option 1: You can simply type an attention-getting phrase followed by your name, title, and the name of the organization. Here's an example of one of my successful subject lines: "Important Information from Dr. Bev Browning, Director–Grant Writing Training Foundation." Option 2: You can capture the recipient's attention with an urgent need subject line such as "26 FAMILIES WITH YOUNG CHILDREN are on the Holiday Cots waiting list...we need your help!" Option 1 legitimizes you as the sender of the e-mail, and Option 2 immediately begins the funding appeal conversation. Both options work very well when it comes to their open rates. Note that I used ALL CAPS in the first few words for Option 2. This shouts to the reader about a very important target population group in dire need. This subject line approach urges the reader to read more and to HELP!

I created an open rate study with 500 Constant Contact e-mail connections. Option 1 was opened by 350 of 500 recipients (a 70 percent open rate); Option 2 was opened by 375 (a 75 percent open rate). This means that they both work. While the 500 contacts had given me their business cards over the past 20 years, none had ever received any e-mails from me until this study.

2. Opening Personalization Line. This is where you address the e-mail reader directly. "Sarah, did you know that...?" "Mark, our families need your support..." "Jeff, historical works of world-renowned artists are sitting in an unsecured storage area of the museum's basement!" Remember, this is your lead-in line where you connect the organization's need to the e-mail reader's familiar, value-driven area of contribution history (also known as past funding priorities). If you did your homework on Mark, you would have found out that he is married and has six young children. In other words, Mark is a family man and supports organizations that serve families. In Jeff's case, you would have read the online newspaper archives and discovered that he attended several museum openings in the past year and won an auction for a highly coveted historical work of art. Your organization's funding needs must be matched to potential contributors that have value-driven interests in your areas of need.

3. Continuation of the Personalization Line Need. Write four to six bulleted sentences on the need or problem that the contribution will meet or solve. Incorporate statistics and keep your area of need within a past-12-months time frame. Let's pick up on the letter to Mark in the following perfect phrases:

- In the past three months, our emergency shelter for homeless families has been faced with some tough decisions.

- While we've been blessed with room for 26 family-size durable cots, each cold and rainy night, an average of 26 additional Portland homeless families with very young children (ages newborn to three years old) have been turned away due to a lack of cots and space.

- With a predictable cold and damp winter season ahead, it's critical that we raise the funds to expand our space and purchase more family-size cots.

- The building attached to our west wall is empty and meets all code requirements for emergency shelter.

- The landlord has agreed to lease this building to us for $1 a year if we bear the cost of removing the separating wall ($5,000).

- A local cot supplier will reduce the costs of the family-size cots (which sleep two adults and up to three children) to $250 each.

4. Giving Link Line. This is where you embed the link to your organization's website and tell the readers why you're directing them to your site: "Mark, you can help us meet this critical need by making a contribution today at http://www.holidaycots.org."

5. Closing the Fundraising Appeal Line. Close the appeal with a line like the following: "As a family man, I know you can relate to how it must feel to be homeless with a young family living on the streets and depending on the generosity of others to see you through this humiliating, life-altering, seems like a never-ending time in your life." *You'll notice that I ended this in a series of three hard-to-forget descriptors that I want to remain in Mark's mind—driving him to contribute now!*

6. Signing Off Line. Finish your e-mail with one of these closings: *Hopefully* or *Awaiting Your Gift* or *Granting Needs*. Here's an example: "Granting Needs for Portland Families, Bev." Remember, your full name, title, organization, and contact information should be in your e-mail signature line. Keep your signature line professional. If your organization has social media pages on LinkedIn, Facebook, or Twitter (popular social media sites for fundraising), provide embedded icons with direct links for the e-mail reader.

Outline for Postal Mail Fundraising Appeals

Fundraising letters might seem old school or outdated, but they still work and I prefer them over e-mail fundraising appeals. Most funding decision makers (contributors of $1,000 or more per request) are over the age of 50 and still like to read highly personalized paper letters. And it's not just the letter inside the envelope that matters; it's also the envelope! I'll first outline perfect phrases for the letter's contents and then give you directions on the "wrapping" provided by the envelope.

The Contents

The outline of the fundraising letter is similar to the e-mail fundraising appeal; however, the length of the hard-copy letter can be up to three single-spaced pages. Of course, it must be on your organization's letterhead stationery.

1. Date Line. All fundraising letters must have a date line at the top (I recommend you align this flush left rather than centering it). Remember, the day you write the letter will likely not be the day the letter is ready for mailing. Once you've composed the letter, you'll want to have a colleague proof and edit it at least twice. After any changes or corrections have been made, you'll want to read it again to make sure that the changes did not diminish your reading impact intent. Date the letter last, right before you print it, and make sure to mail the letter that day. Remember to use a traditional dateline. For example, use "November 27, 2012," not "11/27/12."

2. Addressee Line. Remember the personalization impact discussed at the beginning of this chapter? The addressee line is where you insert the recipient's full name, professional title, organization's name, and complete address. Here's an example of how to line up the information:

> Mrs. Hilda Conrad
> President
> Conrad Family Fund
> 123456 W. Money Lane, Suite 5467
> Gold Rush, Nebraska 87654

3. Salutation Line. First type *Dear Mrs. Conrad*. Once you've printed the letter, take a felt-tip pen (the one you plan to sign the letter with), cross out *Mrs. Conrad* (use one angled diagonal line), and write in *Hilda*. Why? This personalizes the letter even more! Hilda will think that you've met and that you know her personally. Yes, this is a fundraising tip and trick to get Hilda to read the letter and contribute to your organization.

4. The First or Opening Paragraph. It's important to create a compelling lead line to capture the reader's attention. If you're writing to Hilda to solicit funds for public broadcasting sponsorship, you can lead with something like this: "Hilda, how many times did you watch *Frontline*, our PBS flagship public affairs series, in the past five years? Chances are that Hilda has seen *Frontline* at least once or even stopped to view it for a few minutes while channel surfing. How do you know this? Because when you did your initial prospect research on Hilda, you discovered that she contributed to a PBS tele-fundraiser during a *Frontline* episode. Remember, research is the mainstay of fundraising appeal success! Continue your writing with a factual statement about how many sponsors it takes to produce one episode of *Frontline*, like this: "Did you know that it takes 5,000 sponsors at the $100 level to produce one episode of *Frontline*? Larger contributors reduce the number of sponsors needed and free up our limited financial resources to allocate funding for additional episodes. Thanks to viewers like you, Hilda, *Frontline* has been one of PBS's top viewed shows for 10 years. First, I want to thank you for your patronage. Second, I want to share a few facts about the behind-the-scenes expenses involved with producing *Frontline*:"

● Broadcast journalist (1) at an average per episode cost of $200,000.

- Crew members (10) at an average per episode cost of $250,000.
- Promotions at an average per episode cost of $50,000.

5. The Second Paragraph. Introduce your organization. If you're a PBS affiliate station, give your station's identification or moniker and the year it was started. For example, "AZ-PBS, Channel 9, Arizona, started broadcasting in 1982." (This shows that your organization is not new and has longevity in operating on the air.) Next, link your organization to the potential contributor. For example, "Hilda, AZ-PBS works hard to bring you programming of value and interest. The Robert Burns Jazz Series caught your attention, and you received one of our free CD packages as a thank-you for your monetary gift. *Frontline* is one of your favorites; we know this because you've been one of our largest faithful annual contributors."

6. The Third Paragraph. This is where you recall the problem that funding will solve. Don't repeat the same sentences that you wrote in the first paragraph, just remind the reader of the critical nature of the problem. For example, "Hilda, in this economy AZ-PBS is struggling to keep quality programming on the air. Losing a series like *Frontline* would create a viewer void in our public affairs series lineup."

7. The Fourth Paragraph. You can either make the appeal with the amount of funding needed or make an open appeal leaving the funding amount to the letter's recipient. For example, "A $5,000 contribution represents 1/100 of *Frontline*'s production expenses" or "Any contribution toward our massive production expenses is greatly appreciated and will be applied prudently."

8. The Closing. Write a compelling closing line, followed by your signature, title, and work contact information along with a handwritten impacting postscript. For example:

> Anticipating your continuing investment in *Frontline*,
> Dr. Beverly A. Browning
> Development Director
> AZ–PBS
> 480-768-7400 (direct line)
> drbeverlybrowning@gmail.com
> http://www.azpbs.org

P.S. Hilda, the Frontline *journalists and crew are eagerly looking forward to its 13th season on PBS!*

Reminders

Thoroughly research each letter campaign recipient.

Follow the outlines provided for electronic and postal mail appeals.

Personalize every paragraph by using the recipient's first name.

The Wrapping

The best way to capture a potential giver's attention is to enclose your fundraising letter in a bright catalog-size envelope that is hand addressed to the targeted letter reader. The color you choose for your envelope should stand out from the rest of the fundraising letters that we all receive and throw away before opening. Funds that are needed urgently should be in red envelopes; environmental and science projects in green or tan (recycled, of course!); art projects in pastel; education projects in strong bold colors like royal blue or Kelly green or bright orange; public broadcasting projects in gray or black (for black, use a silver felt-tip pen for the hand addressing), and faith-based in sky blue. These are my preference after having tested multiple colors and their impact on recipient psychology in increasing open rates and contribution rates. This study was conducted for nearly five years (I've been doing fundraising for 40 years). I always use a felt-tip pen to hand address the envelopes. Printed commercial return address labels are fine and have no impact over handwritten return address labels. I also add a personal note on the face (addressee side) of the envelope that is meant only for the reader—not a receptionist or mail room staffer. The note, most often, is *URGENT!* or *TIME SENSITIVE!* This captures the recipient's attention. Also, use postage stamps to increase personalization. Select stamps that fit your area of need.

CHAPTER 2

The First Paragraph

As a successful fund developer, I work hard to be creative in each and every fundraising letter campaign. I know that when I read my incoming mail, I look for compelling lead-in language that makes me want to read further. If the first paragraph is not an attention grabber, I'm done with the communication. This is how recipients of your fundraising letters react to boring letters that look like bad chain mail. In other words, everyone wants the recipient's dollar. It's important for you to make your first paragraph personal, impacting, magnetizing, and compelling.

We all want to write about our organization first. This is a fatal error. Introducing your organization too soon can kill the sale or turn off the potential donor. We're also tempted to introduce ourselves by our name and title. Don't make this introductory error either. The first paragraph is the bait (because you're fishing for money). Your bait language must present perfect phrases that cover three key points.

Elements of the First Paragraph

1. Create a Compelling Lead Line.
2. Humanize the Problem.
3. Strengthen Reading Magnetism with Demographics.

1. Create a Compelling Lead Line

Remember, in order to write a compelling lead line, you must personalize it (see Chapter 1). Using the recipient's first name is critical to starting your lead line. Once you address the recipient, you link him or her to your organization's cause or need. Knowing about the professional and personal nuances of the letter recipient helps you make this value-driven connection in the first sentence of your fundraising letter or e-mail. *I can't emphasize enough how important it is for you to use the correct first name or military or honorable title (if applicable), spell it correctly, and know something about each letter's recipient.*

Here are some perfect phrases for lead lines that you can replicate with ease.

- Robert, did you know that St. Matthews Elementary School was built in the same year that you were born?

- Sharon, did you know that over 1,000 children the same age as your 11-year-old twins Sarah and Seth are on the waiting list for a Big Brother or Sister?

- Jeff, I'll bet you never thought that the 100 acres of farm-land tilled by your great-grandparents would become a sprawling megamall endangering adjacent wetlands, did you?

- Emily, the Mathias Avenue Art Museum has a blank frame waiting and ready for the newest Gerhard Richter paint-ing; regretfully, without your sponsorship, this acquisition is beyond our means.

- Andrew, last night the mobile street survival van drove over 400 miles to hand out blankets, bottled water, and knit caps to homeless teens sleeping in alleys, under bridges, and in abandoned properties—some within 5 miles of your neighborhood.

- Mildred, one day the research being conducted by Dr. Jeanette Vann may lead to a cure for Angelman syndrome—a diagnosis shared by over 3,000 children including your nephew, Danny.

- Jeremy, did you know that Georgia Public Broadcasting has something in common with your family?

- Carol, Kansas State University's main campus has fewer automatic electronic defibrillators for our 60,000 students than your building has installed on its 11 floors.

- Marcus, what would you think if I told you that nearly 300 kindergarteners—like your son, Seth—come to school hungry every morning?

- Capt. Mathers, did you know that while you're at Coast Guard duties one weekend a month, approximately 50 returning veterans from Afghanistan and Iraq are coming home to eviction notices and foreclosed homes in our state?

● Judy, it's no coincidence that your neighborhood has three new volunteer crime watch units in training…gang activity is at an all-time high since the County's juvenile detention facility closed!

● Honorable Judge Richardson, last year the Bostwick Volunteer Fire Department traveled down 128 rural roads to save homes, crops, barns, and lives including Spires Road, where we saved 600 acres of soy crops adjacent to your property.

Note: The common thread in these lead lines is that each one implies that we have done our homework to know the first names, proper titles, and link to our causes, organizations, and events. Without this personalization impact, the recipient as no reason to read the rest of our fundraising letter.

2. Humanize the Problem

When I tell you to humanize the problem, I mean for you to introduce written language that brings life to the essence of your problem—the need for funding. If your volunteer team needs sponsors for each mile of the American Cancer Society's Relay for Life walkathon, you have to appeal to individuals that can identify with the need to cure cancer. Telling a brief story about a cancer victim humanizes the disease to a personal viewpoint rather than focusing on the dollars needed for research. Let's continue with the lead lines from the first section of this chapter so you can get the full picture of how to connect several perfect phrase components.

- The aging infrastructure at our elementary school has been cited with multiple code violations including asbestos contamination, mold, and a crumbling facade. In the past three years, the school nurse has recorded 75 cases of undiagnosed asthma (out of 300 children, this is 25 percent), 124 incidents of mold allergies (itching, whelps, and sneezing), and sadly, four children were victims of debris falling off the building and causing minor injuries. Our parents, teachers, support staff, and administrators are frustrated and concerned.

- Among the children waiting to be assigned to a Big Brother or Big Sister are seven sets of twins. Alejandra and Alejandro, 11-year-old fraternal twins, are two of 10 siblings born to a first-generation American family that migrated from Ecuador four years ago sponsored by a local church, the Quijije family. Their Papa has a congenital heart defect that prevents him from working outside of their home (which was provided by the church). The twins are learning English, have made many friends at church and school, and are eager for a Big Brother and Big Sister.

- Last year, over 2 million shoppers descended on the Mall of the Midlands to find sales bargains, eat at a national chain restaurant, attend a movie at the 40-screen Cineplex, or even take in a concert in the outdoor amphitheater. They came in droves via charter buses, cars, trains, and airplanes. The commotion at the mall on a daily basis produces many tons of waste, vehicle exhaust emissions, and extremely high decibels of sound related to vehicle traffic. The airport, just five miles away, has added 20 more flights weekly to accommodate shoppers from out of state and outside of the country. Air quality is at an all-time low according to the latest studies conducted by the Environmental Protection Agency. I'm willing to bet that your great-grandparents (Anna and Jeremiah) never imagined the fate of their land or that the century-old wetlands adjacent to the mall would be endangered and disregarded by commercial developers.

● Your chain of fine art boutiques are frequented by high-profile families such as the Rockefellers, Kennedys, Buffets, and Gates. Internationally, the works of Robert Ryman, Kazemir Malevich, Ad Reinhardt, and Gerhard Richter have been known to find a special place in your highly trafficked locations. Of high interest to our museum Board of Directors are the works of Gerhard Richter. He has often been quoted as his early family life as "simple, orderly, structured—mother playing the piano and the father earning money." Our generation, pre-Depression, holds these same fond memories. Consider the delight that will be created throughout the western world if by chance our museum is gifted one of his paintings for all to admire.

● I'll bet you're wondering why teens are living on the streets in our community. Well, based on our nightly conversations with them, they are living on the streets for three primary reasons: (1) Abused and neglected by parents and foster parents and tired of the system that had made them victims. (2) Both parents are dead or incarcerated or missing in action (simply walked away) and they have no kin to take them in. (3) Undocumented immigrants afraid to seek help from social services agencies; they were smuggled into the United States without their parents and ran away from agricultural servant-like conditions where they were working to pay for their transportation. These teens depend on human angels; they do not steal or terrorize the neighborhoods where they live (there are three encampments six traffic lights away from your home).

● Children with Angelman syndrome typically have a happy, excitable demeanor with frequent smiling, laughter, and hand-flapping movements. Hyperactivity, a short attention span, and a fascination with water are common. Most affected children also have difficulty sleeping and need less sleep than usual. While there is no specific therapy for Angelman syndrome, medical therapy for seizures is usually necessary. Physical and occupational therapies, communication therapy, and behavioral therapies are important in allowing individuals with Angelman syndrome to reach their maximum developmental potential. This year, Dr. Vann is conducting research on neurogenic disorders in six children to develop techniques to diagnose, treat, prevent, and ultimately cure them.

● As parents, our roles are to create nurturing environments to raise our children in; produce offspring that are givers rather than takers in this life; and educate our sons and daughters on responsible citizenship practices. Our roles closely align with the mission of Georgia Public Broadcasting: To create, produce, and distribute high quality programs and services that educate, inform, and entertain our audiences and enrich the quality of their lives. Our biggest fans are parents like you and Jenny. Our family-oriented programming brings *A Place of Our Own*, *Biz Kid$*, and *Count on It* into homes across Georgia including yours. Parents like us know that quality entertainment is not just video games or movie surfing, right?

● Can an automatic electronic defibrillator (AED) at the right place at the right time make a difference? You bet! These portable wall-mounted devices have found their way into every public facility worldwide. One of our volunteers works in your building, several floors away from your offices. She did a walk-through and counted four in each of the four wings on all 11 floors. Wow, Carol, that's a total of 176 AEDs in your building. It must be comforting to know that if you or one of your colleagues has a cardiac arrest that help is just a few feet away from any office. Our campus has only one per building in each of the 20 multistory buildings. With 60,000 students and 4,500 employees, we're all walking a thin line when it comes to actually finding and using an AED.

● Breaking the fast, or *breakfast* as we've all come to call our morning meal, is a critical beginning intended to end eight or more hours of sleep with no food intake. Um, pretty basic and a no-brainer, right? No, it's not so basic to the working poor and chronically unemployed families whose children attend school with Seth. Seth's class and schoolmates are all not lucky enough to have a warm dinner before being sent to bed hungry. Our dedicated teachers have been bringing in fruit, granola bars, and cartons of milk to provide the needed brain fuel to their small charges. It's a struggle at best.

● Jeff, Mary, Richard, Eileen, Connie, Justin, and Wendy are the names of just a handful of returning young and disabled veterans that came home to our community and found out that they were no longer homeowners. After having served our country and dealing with loss of limb— and in some cases family members (through divorce or death)—these proud American citizens have found themselves homeless. Do you remember when you first came back from full-time Coast Guard duty, Capt. Mathers? As one of the more fortunate military family members, you came back to a home full of life and love. The support system designed for returning veterans was working then…

● The closure of this facility has resulted in incarcerated youth being returned to our community. Their families (mostly single-parent nonworking households) do not have the resources to provide the rigorous aftercare services needed for their sudden transition. I'm sure that you've read in the local newspaper that many of these youth are still angry, frightened, and now they feel abandoned by the system that was supposed to house them from entry through rehabilitation. The six nonsecure detention homes in the county have waiting lists that are at least three years long. These kids are on the streets, and the level of concern by our community's stakeholders is high.

● When the fire alarm sounds, over 20 dedicated community servants much like you, Honorable Judge Richardson, report to the station knowing that one of the following dire circumstances could occur: (1) The 20-year old pumper truck may not start. (2) The protective gear they need to wear when fighting fires is so old that when they are dressing, some of the jackets and pants or boots may be so dry-rotted that they will tear once they come in contact with body heat or as they are pulled on. (3) The miles from the station to the fire may be so hazardous over wet, muddy, rut-filled dirt roads that they may get stuck in the mud and not make it in time to save a family's life or livestock or coveted crops.

3. Strengthen Reading Magnetism with Demographics

In this final sentence or two of the first paragraph, it's important to validate your problem or the funding need. Make sure you do your homework and have up-to-date research on the severity of the problem that funding will solve. When you've added the magnetizing demographics, you're done with this section.

Here are some perfect phrases to end your first paragraph

with while emphasizing the severity of the problem. (These examples continue with the same organizations introduced in the first section of this chapter.)

- According to the Centers for Disease Control (CDC), 10 to 12 percent of children are diagnosed with asthma; for the children in our school, it's 25 percent! One in four Americans have mold allergies; again our children surpass the national average (41 percent of our entire enrollment are being treated).

- It's a proven fact that Big Brothers Big Sisters works. A child who is mentored by a big brother or a big sister is 40 percent less likely to get into trouble and 75 percent more likely to be confident, successful, and happy.

- Commercially emitted pollution has contaminated 18 million acres of lakes, estuaries, and wetlands nationwide.

- While the museum holds title to over 1,800 highly valuable artifacts and paintings, the one highly sought-after painting by Richter represents, in monetary value, 20 percent of our current inventory. Research shows that holding a Richter will increase our admission revenues by 40 percent.

- According to our local police department, 20 percent of teens living on the streets are victims of rape, robbery, and assault.

- One in 20,000 children are diagnosed with Angelman syndrome. This means that annually 13 of the estimated

200,000 children born in the United States will be diagnosed with this mystery disease.

- Some 200,000 PBS viewers in Georgia have young children that are likely to view one or more of our adolescent-directed programs weekly. The cost to deliver quality programs like those listed above is $30,000 per day.

- According to a study by the Kansas Medical Journal, only 50 percent of the state's college campuses (19 sites) have AEDs installed. Looking closely at those 19 sites, institutions with 15 to 20 buildings have at least 4 to 6 AEDs per building.

- Research shows that one out of three kindergarten-age children come to school hungry.

- Two hundred thousand veterans are returning to the U.S. this year. In our state, 200 veterans are now homeless.

- Nassau County has 275 Persons In Need of Supervision (PIN) that are without psychological counseling. One hundred percent of these youth are former gang members and at high risk of committing additional crimes.

- Last year, our volunteer fire department spent $45,000 on vehicle maintenance. The wear and tear on our pumper and brush trucks reduced their life operation cycle by five years.

CHAPTER 3

The Second Paragraph

This is the paragraph where you introduce your organization, provide accountability information, and insert a bit of well-researched trivia to link your organization with the potential contributor. This paragraph should be a smooth transition from the first paragraph. I recommend two sentences about your organization, two sentences about accountability, and one sentence for the trivia link.

This is the nitty-gritty paragraph that gives the readers up-front information about who is writing to them, the validity of the asking organization, and why the recipient is receiving a fundraising appeal from this specific organization. In other words, the reader wants to read about a connection between something your organization is doing or has done and his or her own interests, life, or values.

Elements of the Second Paragraph

1. Introduce Your Organization.

2. Provide Accountability Information.
3. Link Your Organization to the Potential Contributor.

1. Introduce Your Organization

First, although your organization's fundraising letter will likely be on letterhead stationery, it's still polite to introduce the name of the organization first. Remember to use the legal name found on your Internal Revenue Services (IRS) Letter of Determination for Tax-Exempt Status (more about this later). Some potential contributors may want to look your organization up on Guidestar.com to see if you're listed and have uploaded recent financial statements and IRS Form 990 tax returns (for tax-exempt organizations). Also include the year that your organization was founded.

Second, no one likes to give money to a non-tax-exempt organization. So when you introduce your organization, it's important to indicate your tax-exempt status. Cite the specific Internal Revenue Service code. Figure 3-1 provides a wee bit of a refresher if you're not sure about your specific tax-exempt code (and ask someone at your organization for a copy of the IRS Letter of Determination for Tax-Exempt Status). All of this information should be included in the first sentence.

The second sentence should focus on your services or programs and geographic area(s) covered. Keep the sentence at less than 15 to 20 words. I tend to be a long sentence writer because I don't want to break up the reader's thoughts or concentration.

Here are some perfect phrases to introduce your organization.

Figure 3-1 Types of 501(c) Organizations

According to the IRS Publication 557, in the "Organization Reference Chart" section, the following is an exact list of 501(c) organization types and their corresponding descriptions.

- 501(c)(1)—Corporations Organized Under Act of Congress (including Federal Credit Unions)
- 501(c)(2)—Title Holding Corporation for Exempt Organization
- 501(c)(3)—Religious, Educational, Charitable, Scientific, Literary, Testing for Public Safety, to Foster National or International Amateur Sports Competition, or Prevention of Cruelty to Children or Animals Organizations
- 501(c)(4)—Civic Leagues, Social Welfare Organizations, and Local Associations of Employees
- 501(c)(5)—Labor, Agricultural, and Horticultural Organizations
- 501(c)(6)—Business Leagues, Chambers of Commerce, Real Estate Boards, etc.
- 501(c)(7)—Social and Recreational Clubs
- 501(c)(8)—Fraternal Beneficiary Societies and Associations
- 501(c)(9)—Voluntary Employee Beneficiary Associations
- 501(c)(10)—Domestic Fraternal Societies and Associations
- 501(c)(11)—Teachers' Retirement Fund Associations
- 501(c)(12)—Benevolent Life Insurance Associations, Mutual Ditch or Irrigation Companies, Mutual or Cooperative Telephone Companies, etc.
- 501(c)(13)—Cemetery Companies
- 501(c)(14)—State-Chartered Credit Unions, Mutual Reserve Funds
- 501(c)(15)—Mutual Insurance Companies or Associations
- 501(c)(16)—Cooperative Organizations to Finance Crop Operations
- 501(c)(17)—Supplemental Unemployment Benefit Trusts
- 501(c)(18)—Employee Funded Pension Trust (created before June 25, 1959)
- 501(c)(19)—Post or Organization of Past or Present Members of the Armed Forces
- 501(c)(21)—Black Lung Benefit Trusts
- 501(c)(22)—Withdrawal Liability Payment Fund
- 501(c)(23)—Veterans Organization (created before 1880)
- 501(c)(25)—Title Holding Corporations or Trusts with Multiple Parents
- 501(c)(26)—State-Sponsored Organization Providing Health Coverage for High-Risk Individuals
- 501(c)(27)—State-Sponsored Workers' Compensation Reinsurance Organization
- 501(c)(28)—National Railroad Retirement Investment Trust

Source link: IRS, Publication 557 "Tax-Exempt Status for Your Organization," pp. 65–66, (Rev. June 2008), Cat. No 46573C, IRS.gov, accessed January 27, 2009.

(I am continuing with the organizations that were used in the perfect phrases examples in Chapters 1 and 2.)

- St. Matthews Elementary School was founded in 1948 and holds IRS 501(c)(3) tax-exempt status under the Archdiocese of Los Angeles. Our school is located in south central Los Angeles (considered blighted inner city) and serves 300 primarily Hispanic children in grades K–8.

- Big Brothers Big Sisters of America—a 501(c)(3) nonprofit—formed in 1977 when Big Brothers Association and Big Sisters International joined forces and became Big Brothers Big Sisters of America. The Tucson chapter mentors over 1,000 children from throughout southern Arizona and has the largest database of bilingual mentors and children in the western region.

- Save the Wetlands Trust, Inc., a 501(c)(5) nonprofit agricultural/environmental organization, was founded in 2005 in an effort to preserve, protect, and restore endangered wetlands. For the next 20 years, our efforts are focused on North America; specifically, wetland areas that are adjacent to over-commercialized mega-properties like the Mall of the Midlands, which is five miles from our headquarters in Omaha, Nebraska.

- The Mathias Avenue Art Museum Foundation is a 501(c)(3) private operating foundation started with an inheritance from Arthur and Mary Mathias upon their joint deaths in 2000. Located in Vale, Colorado, the museum is visited by patrons worldwide who come for special viewings, art education forums, art auctions, and our famous Jazz on the Rocks–Art on the Side series held in the outdoor garden the first Sunday of each month.

● Helping Wheels, Inc. was incorporated in 1982 when the number of teens living on the streets escalated; we are a 501(c)(3) IRS-approved tax-exempt nonprofit organization. Our mobile street survival vans (six in operation) cover 40 square miles in and surrounding Sunset, Florida, an upscale suburban mid- to upper-income community of 40,000 multigenerational residents.

● Named after Dr. Harry Angelman, the Angelman Syndrome Research Institute was founded in 1965 as a 501(c)(3) nonprofit organization. Based in Bend, Oregon, the Institute conducts revolutionary research that supports a higher quality of life for afflicted children and adults.

● Georgia Public Broadcasting Media, Inc. is a 501(c)(3) listener-supported public radio network incorporated in 1975. Strategically located in Atlanta, Georgia Public Broadcasting's nine public television stations deliver quality PBS and locally produced programming to every county in Georgia and to significant portions of surrounding states.

● The Kansas State University Foundation is a 501(c)(3) nonprofit entity founded in 1944 as the institution's official fundraising arm. Guided by a strong commitment to our stakeholders including students, faculty, and partners in and adjacent to our Manhattan, Kansas, campus, our mission is to aggressively work to strengthen institutional resources including campus facilities.

- The Navajo Nation School District is a federally recognized 501(c)(3) reservation-based public school district for Navajo children. Among the 20 K–12 schools serving the Navajo Nation in the Four Corners region of the United States (Arizona, Colorado, New Mexico, and Utah), Flaming Warriors Elementary Schools is based in Kayenta, Arizona, and provides culturally relevant educational programming to nearly 7,000 students in kindergarten through eighth grades.

- The Home Soon Promise was founded in 2009 and is a 501(c)(3) nonprofit charitable organization managed by disabled and formerly homeless/chronically unemployed returning veterans from Afghanistan and Iraq. Based in Long Beach, California, our new home and job relocation service areas extend throughout all of southern California covering seven counties (Los Angeles, Orange, Riverside, San Bernardino, San Diego, Santa Barbara, and Ventura).

- Leadership Training Institute is a minority-founded 501(c)(3) nonprofit charitable organization founded in 1973 by a national activist, Mel Jackson. Based in Hempstead, New York, our services include operating two nonsecure residential detention homes for adjudicated youth; GED completion for high school dropouts; juvenile job training and placement; and aftercare services for youth discharged from secure and nonsecure detention facilities throughout Long Island.

- The Friends of the Bostwick Volunteer Fire Department formed a 501(c)(3) IRS-approved nonprofit tax-exempt organization in 2002 shortly after the massive tornado devastation that took lives, livestock, and property. We were formed to help the 100 percent volunteer county fire department raise the funds needed to better serve our residents in rural and remote Lancaster County, Pennsylvania.

2. Provide Accountability Information

You have one first chance to establish your organization's accountability to potential donors. By this, I mean that you must write at least two sentences about the organization's capability to prudently and cost-effectively manage donor contributions. With thousands of scams uncovered weekly in the nonprofit sector (the heart of fundraising), it's critical to show a line of strong and reliable accountability beginning with your board of directors and ending with audited financial statements available for review, if requested.

I also think it's wise to include a sentence about the percentage of your funds that are allocated to direct services for programming, events, or causes. I'm going to continue the storylines you're been reading in the following perfect phrases so you can connect the dots with an entire letter for each type of organization profiled.

Here are the perfect phrases examples for the second paragraph. Reminder, only write two sentences!

● St. Matt (our nickname) is managed by a 12-member Parent Advisory Board that includes homemakers, blue-collar workers, and white-collar professionals. The Board has established a $50,000 endowment fund (100 percent of the interest is reinvested back into the school's scholarship fund). In addition, the Diocese provides contracted CPA services to produce our annual financial report (available for review on request); to date, we have not had any negative audit findings.

● The Tucson chapter of Big Brothers Big Sisters is governed by a 20-member regional Board of Directors that represents every segment of the stakeholder community. Each chapter is audited by the national parent organization annually and by regional business managers to assure that 90 percent of all fundraising revenues are directed to programming.

● Save the Wetlands Trust is managed by a six-member international Board of Advisors that meet via Skype monthly to review management progress reports and examine financial statements. In addition, the Trust's funds are managed by the National Bank of Canada with investments monitored by maximum returns (95 percent of all contributions are allocated to our mission).

● When the Mathias family willed their estate assets to our Museum, we formed a 10-member Government Board that includes two family members, a CPA, a tax attorney, an international art historian, a former Sweden Museum of Contemporary Art procurement consultant, and two major donors that have given over $1 million each to the

Foundation. Approximately 80 percent of all funds raised are allocated for the museum's ongoing collection and maintenance expenses.

- Helping Wheels has a 30-member publicly connected Board of Directors that represent County housing, employment and training, homeless shelters, social services, public health, law enforcement, and fire services (EMTs). Ninety cents of every dollar donated goes to help teens survive in the streets; our accounting is managed by the largest CPA firm in Florida.

- The Institute's Managing Board is composed of 12 single-disease medical researchers from throughout the world. Finances are managed prudently and cost effectively by a third-party trust officer from the World Bank; 100 percent of all funds raised are used to support Angelman syndrome research.

- Our seven-member Board of Directors at Georgia Public Broadcasting Media, Inc., represents television and radio sectors of Georgia broadcast venues including members from major national cable television corporations. Our finances are under continual scrutiny due to the number of telethons and resulting pledges from viewers who see 80 cents of every dollar used for programming expenses; no negative audit findings have ever been reported in our 36 year history.

- The Foundation's dedicated Board of Directors includes former alumni, retired deans, and a previous two-term governor. The Institutional Infrastructure Fund is managed by Merrill Lynch Financial Management; 95 percent of contributions are redirected toward campus improvements.

- The Navajo Nation School District is governed by a 40-member multistate Board of Education that oversees the management aspect and monitors student outcomes for our massive student body. A federally approved financial management system has been in place for nearly 50 years to ensure that dollars earmarked for Native American education are spent within the guidelines of the Nation and our federal treaty.

- The Home Soon Promise's Board of Directors (12 stellar veterans) are previous clients that have received services from our organization. Finances are managed by a former U.S. Department of Veteran Affairs Financial Officer who monitors the funding allocation percentage closely (99 percent of all contributions are used to help clients).

- The 10-member Board of Directors oversees the Executive Director's daily management of our organization. Annual CPA-certified audits are conducted, as well as grantor agency financial audits (for over 100 grants) which have never found any questionable costs (90 cents of every dollar is allocated to programming).

- Our volunteer five-member Board of Directors reflects the local agricultural community, and the directors are dedicated to maintaining the integrity of our Pennsylvania Amish beliefs. The local bank, Amish Village Trust and Savings, oversees all donations coming into the Friends of the Bostwick Volunteer Fire Department (100 percent of funds are used to support operating expenses).

3. Link Your Organization to the Potential Contributor

Seasoned fundraisers will tell you to write concise sentences and not to offer any nonessential language. Firsthand experience has shown me that if anyone is going to give you money, it's because something you've written has struck a memory or value in his or her mind or heart. This won't happen if you just stick to the boring facts about what your organization needs and what it has accomplished. Fundraising is about storytelling. By this, I mean you must include components within your letter or e-mail narratives that clearly link the funder with your organization, cause, event, and, most important, its need.

End the second paragraph with a trivia point that readdresses the reader. This paragraph-ending sentence is needed to drive the funder to want to read the rest of your letter. (Remember, I'm continuing with the same 12 agencies so you can see the complete picture of these perfectly phrased fundraising letters and e-mails.)

Here are the clincher connector sentences that speak directly to the reader.

- Robert, I just checked the yearbooks and realized that you attended St. Matthews for second through fourth grades!

- Sharon, our volunteer coordinator just sent me a note that your sister and sister-in-law are both Big Sisters in our chapter!

- Jeff, family legacy is everything; I wonder if your Grandpa's ducks have offspring nesting in the wetlands.

- Emily, I looked at your family lineage on ancestry.com and see that you have two relatives on your mother's side of the family with the last name of Mathias; perhaps our street—and museum—carries their name.

- Andrew, I know that you work for Langley Bank and Trust and that your route to and from work likely is the same route that our mobile street survival van takes nightly.

- Mildred, Danny has a chance at a better quality of life if he is accepted into Dr. Van's next study group.

- Jeremy, we know that generations of McDonalds worked in logging across Georgia—one of the sites is where our studio sits in Fulton County—and that their hard work helped to form your youngest generation's family values.

- Carol, how does it feel to have three generations of Kansas State University graduates in your immediate family?

- Marcus, I'm sure that your grandparents have passed down oral history about the difficulties that families faced feeding their children and themselves during the Great Depression.

- Capt. Mathers, I'm sure that many a returning veteran would like to know how you managed to come back from Afghanistan (first tour) and Iraq (second and third tours) with your finances still intact.

- Judy, did you know that the aftercare programs in Long Island keep juvenile delinquents off the streets and out of neighborhoods like yours and mine?

- Honorable Judge Richardson, remember when you and your wife prepared a cooler full of lemonade for our exhausted volunteers after they fought the soy crop fire next door to you?

CHAPTER 4

The Third Paragraph

At this point, the target of your fundraising letter or e-mail has been reading the *grab your attention* paragraphs. Now it's time to coral the readers' focus back to the reason you are writing to them. In this third paragraph, you must draw the readers' attention back to the problem that you will solve with their contribution.

Why do your readers need to be reminded? Because typical adult readers don't read previously written lines of text; instead, they read from top to bottom and then make a decision: to contribute or not contribute. This is why the order of information in your fundraising letters is so critical to getting the readers' attention and keeping them on focus about the reason for the letter.

First, in this chapter, I give you a list of buzzwords that I refer to as eye candy for the readers. These descriptive but memorable words will help you change up your fundraising language in the problem recall paragraph.

Second, in this chapter, I give you perfect phrases for the next attention-grabbing paragraph for your award-winning fundraising letters and e-mails.

Elements of the Third Paragraph

1. Dynamic Buzzwords to Jump-Start Your Ideas and Writing in the Third Paragraph.
2. Recalling the Problem That the Funding Will Solve.

1. Dynamic Buzzwords to Jump-Start Your Ideas and Writing in the Third Paragraph

First, I am giving you the list of all lists for buzzwords (terms to drive the giving mode). You'll see these same buzzwords incorporated into the perfect phrases in the next section in this chapter where I give you the award-winning third paragraph for your fundraising letters and e-mails. Review, consider, incorporate, and wait for the results!

- Appalled
- Bare
- Barriers
- Bombarded
- Chopping
- Chronic

- Collapse
- Compassionate
- Concerns
- Crippling
- Critically
- Dangers

- Dealing
- Delay
- Depend
- Desperate
- Destruction
- Difference
- Disappointed
- Downward
- Eliminate
- Endangered
- Evaporating
- Excuses
- Extinct
- Facing
- Fatality
- Fault
- Foreclosure
- Forever
- Forgotten
- Gripping
- Hazmat-filled
- Impact
- Increased
- Insurmountable

- Lacking
- Lax
- Less
- Lifetime
- Lose
- Luring
- Myriad
- Nearly
- Nonexistent
- Potential
- Preserve
- Promising
- Radiating
- Rally
- Reactive
- Recession
- Recidivism
- Scurry
- Severe
- Severity
- Shortcomings
- Soars
- Spiraling
- Stalls

- Stripped
- Sudden
- Suffering
- Unemployment
- Violence
- Waiting
- Without

2. Recalling the Problem That the Funding Will Solve

Refresh your memory. In Chapter 2, you learned how to human-ize the problem in the second paragraph of your fundraising letters and e-mails. Now, we're going to draw from the initial problem introduced to the reader and write one more compel-ling reminder sentence about the severity of the problem.

When you write this paragraph, stop and reflect on the issues that need funding. Write up two or four sentences that emit gloom, doom, drama, and trauma if funding is not received expeditiously! Remember to remind the funders that their help is needed. (To continue the fluidity of my examples in each chap-ter, the following perfect phrases pick up on the same 12 orga-nizations and connect the dots in the sequence of information.) Here are the perfect phrases for the third paragraph:

- St. Matt children did not ask for the illnesses that our hazmat-filled building is causing. Infrastructure repair funds, an area where we need your help, are nonexis-tent. The severity of our contamination issues is taking St. Matt children from what was once a promising future to one of myriad health concerns—that will likely last a lifetime.

- With so many children waiting for a Big Brother or Big Sister and no funding to launch a community education and awareness campaign aimed at reaching potential adult mentors, I'm afraid that children like Alejandra and Alejandro will be disappointed for another long year. Being on the waiting list for a mentor for even a few months can seem like forever for young children desperate for some one-on-one time with a caring adult. I am hoping that there is a way that you can help our chapter eliminate this waiting list.

- The commercial developers that scooped up your family's ancestral land have turned their backs on the environmental impact to the adjacent wetlands. If we don't team together to preserve what's left of the endangered species and plant life, what will be left for our children to visit and learn from besides getting to the mall—at all costs—to shop, see a movie, or grab a snack? Who else will step up and take a stand on the gentle balance between humans and nature? Without your help, eventually the Mall of the Midlands will become the *Maul of the Midlands* with many of nature's creations suffering and become extinct.

- Lacking the funds to acquire a black-and-white canvas of a highly revered black-and-white artist like Gerhard Richter reflects the hard times that have bombarded art museums like ours. First there were federal funding cuts, followed by a crippling recession that stripped the resources of art lovers who at one time had the means to support our acquisition expenses. We know that you would love to be a partner in acquiring one of Richter's *48 Portraits*, a pantheon of black-and-white headshots depicting male, mostly European leaders in cultural and scientific fields—Alban Berg, Franz Kafka, Albert Einstein.

● What's the difference between a handout and a hand up for the homeless teens living near your neighborhood? If you give them a handout, they'll never see the dangers of living on the streets and likely stay there until they die from violence or illness. If you give them a hand up, it means that you're willing to invest in our mobile counseling services program—not yet started due to a lack of funding—and help us help them get off of the streets.

● Research has shown that children with this syndrome can live a long life. Granted, without additional medical research findings, their lives will be filled with insurmountable mobility, communication, and behavioral barriers. We need compassionate believers in the work that we are doing, and I think that you're a candidate for understanding and supporting our cause. Hundreds of children like Danny will benefit.

● The finances for public broadcasting programming in Georgia feel as if they've simply taken a severe drop from the past five years. We know that our historical contributors are facing unemployment, foreclosure, and joining the ranks of America's evaporating middle class. It is during these hard times that Georgia's PBS family must rally and step up to save children's programming from the chopping block. Children, of all people, should not have to lose the educational values gained from our premium parent-approved series.

● The medical profession says that when we're having a heart attack, it might feel like mild indigestion or like a vice gripping our heart or even like one of our arms has gone to sleep (a radiating sort of pain). Imagine being at work or in a classroom on our campus and having a sudden onslaught of pain right before we collapse from cardiac arrest. I know that it's something that neither one of us wants to have happen to us personally, to anyone that we know and love, or even to one of our bright leaders of the future, KSU students. Carol, it's better to be proactive by purchasing and installing the critically needed AEDs than it is to be reactive once a campus fatality has occurred and the news media run away with the headlines about our emergency medical shortcomings.

● Public schools can no longer depend on federal aid to take care of the nutritional needs of America's children. It's sad, but true. Uncle Sam's coffer for school-provided hot breakfasts is nearly as bare as Old Mother Hubbard's cupboard. Our children don't want excuses or explanations; they want to come to school ready to learn. It is not their fault that their parents and caregivers are dealing with less and less help and income by the minute. Marcus, I guess the buck stops here—in our local community—where every dollar contributed actually makes it to the school's checking account and is allocated 100 percent for the First Morning Nutrition Program.

● Not too long ago, I visited my sister in Natchez, Mississippi, who told me that nearly 200 homeless Vietnam veterans had been living in an encampment in the deep pine forest for at least 35 to 40 years. I was just as appalled to hear this as I know you are to read about the Vietnam War's forgotten soldiers. Capt. Mathers, we can't let this happen to our returning veterans from Afghanistan and Iraq! It's time to step up and address the chronic homelessness facing Southern California's returning veterans and their families.

● What's the impact of putting juvenile offenders back into the community with no follow-up support services? Increased local crime; increased gang growth and destruction; increased youth hanging around on former school grounds luring children like ours to try out drugs, stealing, or gang life; and increased stress on the adult correctional system when their recidivism soars! We, yes you and I, Judy, can make a difference in the life of a young person whose life has gone astray. WE can stop the downward spiraling fall of their precious youth years with the right interventions.

● The fire alarm sounds and nearly a dozen fathers, mothers, sisters, brothers, and other loved ones and neighbors leave their homes and jobs to head for the fire station.

Once they arrive, there is a scurry to find protective gear that is still wearable—a critical time delay for fire that is miles away across hill and dale. Finally ready to roll out, the pumper truck stalls and the engine is flooded. Wasn't this truck just in repair last week? What are WE going to do?

CHAPTER 5

The Fourth Paragraph

This chapter is about writing the fourth and final paragraph in your fundraising letters and e-mails. This is the paragraph where you make the funding appeal to potential contributors.

The first type of appeal examples will include the amount of funding needed and tell funders how their contribution will be used to solve the problem or meet the need. The second type of appeal will leave the funding amount up to the letter or e-mail recipient. This more casual open appeal can result in surprises or disappointments. It's a chance that fund developers must take when they are not sure of the giving capacity of a contributor. If your funding appeal's recipient has a significant amount of discretionary monies, the incoming check could be phenomenal.

However, if you've given the impression that any amount, no matter how small, will make a difference, the more prudent recipients might limit their check to $50. For a small nonprofit in need of mentoring supplies, this is a windfall, but to a large nonprofit needing hundreds of thousands of dollars, this is a major disappointment. Of course, the choice of a specific funding request or an open appeal is up to you and the time frame for your organization's monetary needs.

Note that there is no recommended length for this paragraph. You have up to three pages for four single-spaced paragraphs. This final paragraph is your last chance to close the deal. Write to your heart's content, but don't overdo it!

Elements of the Fourth Paragraph

1. Make the Appeal with the Amount of Funding Needed.
2. Make an Open Appeal Leaving the Funding Amount to the Letter or E-mail Recipient.

1. Make the Appeal with the Amount of Funding Needed

Early on in this book, I emphasized the importance of doing extensive research on your fundraising letter or e-mail recipients. Understanding their level of giving ability is critical to determining how much to ask for in the form of contributions. Once you know if a funder can give your organization a specific amount of money, it also tells you how many of the fundraising appeals you will need to send out in order to capture 100 percent of your contribution goals. (In keeping with the theme of Part One, "Perfect Phrases for Fundraising Letter Campaigns," I'm going to continue with the 12 agencies you've become familiar with in the previous chapters.)

Note: If you did not use the recipient's first name in the third paragraph, start by addressing the individual by his or her name in this fourth paragraph.

Here are the perfect phrases for making an appeal with the specific amount of funding needed included in the final paragraph of your letters and e-mails.

● Robert, would you be willing to contribute $1,000 for each of the three years that you attended St. Matt? Your total gift of $3,000 will help our volunteer Building Fund Committee budget for the first phase of asbestos removal in classroom #9. When you were a student here, Mrs. Ran taught math in #9. I am enclosing a prestamped envelope for your convenience. Oh, you probably won't believe this, but St. Matt has moved into the 21st century when it comes to electronics; we now accept all major credit cards for contributions. You can even pledge a monthly amount, and we will automatically charge your card on the first of each month.

● Sharon, we critically need your help in hiring a part-time Mentoring Coordinator to work on mentoring matches and monitoring for the children on the waiting list. The cost of the Coordinator's annual stipend is $16,000. I'm asking you to reflect a long time and then consider contributing $1,000 toward these unplanned and unbudgeted expenses. We're on a critical deadline and your gift is needed by December 31 in order to start the New Year off with hope and strive to make an impact in the life of each child who is without a mentor. Please make your check payable to our chapter. I've enclosed a prestamped envelope for your convenience.

● Jeff, we're at the crossroads when it comes to preserving the wetlands, and the ecological clock is ticking. With each lost minute, the environmental impact increases. Save the Wetlands Trust, Inc., needs you as a financial stakeholder. Your great-grandparents would be proud! Your donation of $25,000 will boot our preservation fund to the next level. I'd like to call you and set up an appointment to take you on a jeep tour of our wetlands. When you see what has happened and how hard our volunteers are working to restore this habitat, I know you'll want to end the tour by making a gift of the critically needed funds. I'm excited at the possibilities, and so are the new ducklings!

● Emily, I know that you're aware of the rather high bidding wars over a Gerhard Richter black-and-white canvas. The coveted painting that our museum is seeking will likely be auctioned off between $2.2 million and $5 million in the next six months. If we are able to secure 100 percent of the funds ($5 million to be safe), our Acquisitions Director will be able to register and participate in telephone or Internet bidding on one of the paintings up for auction. Richter's last three black-and-white canvases went for an average of $3.5 million. Our Founder's Board is inviting you to our Saturday auction strategy meeting at 9 a.m. on

September 7 where we hope you'll make a commitment to help us acquire one of Richter's works. This will certainly be a dream come true for our museum, the art world, and especially for the Tourism Bureau in Vale, which is ready to promote this new acquisition as a new and *must see* international visitor attraction.

● Andrew, the cost of hiring a part-time mobile counselor is $20,000 a year. You are one of 20 trusted friends of homeless teens that I'm counting on to step up and support this *close to home* critical need. Can we count on you, Andrew? If so, I'm hoping you'll use the enclosed prestamped envelope to make your first annual pledge to help our youth get off of the streets.

● Mildred or Aunt Mildred is likely what Danny calls you, so I hope you don't mind if I call you Aunt Mildred too! You represent one of very few family members that have experienced firsthand the worried looks on everyone's face when Danny was diagnosed. An entire family likely rallied around to help Danny and his parents face medical professionals and question this rare diagnosis. Now that the initial crisis has passed, there's a way to keep on helping other children like Danny—and even adults diagnosed with Angelman syndrome—by financially supporting our medical research. A gift of $500 will support one day of research work. Don't forget, we're going to try to get Danny in our study!

● Jeremy, you can help us continue quality children's programming. How? By making a $2,500 pledge, you can help us keep *family values content* on the air for Georgia's children. Our call center volunteers are on standby from 7 a.m. to 12 midnight seven days a week and are waiting for your call to 1-800-888-8888. It's as easy as a phone call; yes, Jeremy, one person can make a difference and it's you!

● The financial pacemaker at KSU is at a near standstill. Your contribution can be the voltage charger needed to kick off the AEDs Everyplace fundraising campaign. $800 will help us to purchase a HeartStart Onsite Automatic Electronic Defibrillator. We're asking you to help us purchase five (5) AEDs for the KSU campus. I'm enclosing a donation form and prestamped envelope. We can't do this without you!

● We can't feed our children without your help. It's come down to buying books or buying food. Since school is about education, the Board has only approved the funds needed to equipment classrooms, not the stomachs of hungry children. Can you come to the rescue by making a $250 contribution to support the First Morning Nutrition Program at Flaming Warrior Elementary School? I'm embarrassed to write this, but we don't even have the money to spare an envelope or stamp to carry your gift back to our mailbox. I know that you understand our situation and that you'll step up to help!

● Just when it looks like no one cares about the plight of returning veterans facing chronic homelessness, we found you! Please help your comrades by considering a $2,000 contribution for the Home Soon Promise. We can't do this alone, and you're a critical stakeholder on our team. When you're ready (we hope that's soon), please stop by the old National Guard Armory on First Street any day between 8 a.m. and 8 p.m. to talk to our volunteers and drop off your check.

● Leadership Training Institute is boxed into a corner, and the only way out is to ask our friends for financial assistance. Your contribution of $1,000 will pay for one week of aftercare counseling services for 20 high-risk youth. This week is just the beginning of their transition support services when they arrive back into our community. Can we count on you to become one of our long-term financial partners? I'm enclosing a prestamped envelope in hopes that your gift will arrive in time to start the first round of counseling before the end of the year.

● The Friends of Bostwick Fire Department is looking for another friend. If you have a vested interested in our farming community and a deep desire to restore high-quality first responder services, then you're a first place candidate for becoming a friend! Our small friends group would like to hold our next monthly meeting at your farmhouse if that's okay with you. The date and time are flexible, and we'll bring the sweet treats if you'll put on a pot of water for tea bags. Can we count on you for a $7,500 donation to start our pumper truck replacement fund? Oh, we'll talk about the brush truck next year; perhaps at that time you can recommend other potential friends to help us with the cost of this other ready-to-be replaced truck. Thanks, in advance, for joining our group!

2. Make an Open Appeal Leaving the Funding Amount to the Letter or E-mail Recipient

Remember, when you use an open appeal, you're taking a chance on the size of the incoming contribution. You absolutely must know your donor's contributing ability to use this approach.

Here are the perfect phrases for making an open appeal.

- Robert, we know that these are dire economic times for everyone. That's why we don't want to burden you by asking for a specific amount. Instead, I'm asking you to open your heart and check your finances to see how much you can afford to contribute to St. Matt. When the time is right and your faith in our quality education is confirmed, please use the enclosed prestamped envelope to send your contribution toward our asbestos removal fund (averaging around $3,000 per classroom). Thank you, in advance, for any size gift for our children and their safety while in school.

- Sharon, your gift, of any size, will enable our chapter to secure the services of a part-time Mentoring Coordinator. This new and critically needed position will be responsible for matching children with Big Brothers and Big Sisters and conduct ongoing monitoring of match progress. We have a budget of $16,000 for this new staff addition and are starting out with a pledge of $8,000 from our Board of Directors. Can we count on you? If so, please use the enclosed envelope to send your contribution. We're hoping to raise 100 percent of the needed funds by the end of this year. Thank you for remembering what counts in this crazy world of ours.

● Jeff, it's time to stop and look at what is happening to our ecologically precious wetlands and make some hard decisions. Either we're going to take a step forward or many steps backward if we don't act soon. Can you help with this urgency? Your contribution is needed urgently to reverse the damage that has already been done. A small gift from you and other members of your family can create a lasting legacy for your great-grandparents and save what was precious to them at a time when no one dreamed of a megamall on their property and now endangering wildlife and plant life. I'm inclosing a donation form (for credit card gifts) and a prestamped envelope. Time is of the essence, and we're awaiting your positive decision to join our family of preservationists.

● Emily, the average art aficionado could never fathom stepping up and presenting our Founder's Board with a check to cover the cost of a Gerhard Richter black-and-white canvas. Then, you already know that you are above the rest and a longtime patron of our museum and admirer of Richter's 26-piece collection. The auction will be held before we can blink an eye, and if we're not ready to make a competitive bid, our museum, patrons like yourself, and the world at large will lose the opportunity to admire and study one of Richter's paintings in Vale. We're having a meeting on Saturday and a chair will be saved for you. Come ready to listen, reflect on your financial abilities, and then hopefully make a decision to purchase one of his works outright before the end of the year. I'll call you with more specifics on the meeting, time, and so forth.

● Andrew, let's get down to the nitty-gritty. A part-time mobile counselor is going to cost us something that we don't have: $20,000 a year. We're sweating bullets here as the homeless youth population continues to grow. We need you, your colleagues, and your neighbors to have a small community meeting to discuss how you can help us hire this counselor. We're only asking you to look at this one year at a time. We'll certainly look for grant funding after this year once we have the first year of expenses funded. I have some great ideas for how to make this meeting happen. In fact, I can even attend to answer questions if you'd like. Any monetary help from you and other stakeholders will be greatly appreciated.

● Aunt Mildred, children like Danny as well as adults living with a diagnosis of Angelman syndrome need additional life quality–supporting services. Our researchers can continue to release relevant findings to support ongoing care needs. Your contribution can make a difference for thousands of children and adults worldwide. We're asking you to think about Danny's future and then make an investment in our Institute as soon as you can. Please call me when you are ready to invest in our search. We can now accept all major credit cards and e-checks, so you don't even need an envelope, stamp, or paper check. If only the research for Angelman syndrome kept up with today's electronic technology. Maybe one day…

● Jeremy, we can't continue to offer the level of children's programming that we have been without your pledge. A gift of any amount will make a critical difference in our ability to fulfill our mission for Georgia's children. Rather than ask you to call in to our pledge center, I'm enclosing an envelope (with a stamp) for you to return your pledge in. Hurry, the new season starts in a few months. Thanks!

● Our AEDs Everyplace fundraising coffers are bare. We're asking you to help up raise the temperature on the campus's fundraising thermometer. I'm attaching a specifications sheet for the types of AEDs that we need in our buildings. Our Development Office has set up an online donation web page on the KSU Foundation's website. Please consider supporting our campus infrastructure initiative.

● The children are coming to school across many miles, and they are arriving not ready for learning, but too hungry to think. We need your help now more than ever. As a past donor, I personally know of your compassion for our Four Corners Nation. I've enclosed an envelope (sorry, we can't afford the stamps for return mail). Please help us out once more, and we'll find a way to say thanks beyond a traditional note card.

● The troops are coming back home in droves, except they are not returning to the homes they left. Those bank-owned homes are now just shells without these vibrant and dedicated soldiers. The plight of homeless veterans living on the streets is one we must work to solve. We can't do this without your contribution. I've arranged for a special viewing of a video taken right here in our state. It shows what is happening, why it's happening, and how everyone can pitch in and lend a hand. I'm hoping that after our December 1 viewing (8 p.m. at the First Street National Guard Armory), you'll consider leaving a gift of financial love in our Home Soon Promise collection box.

- For nearly 40 years, Leadership Training Institute has been a pathway for leaving poverty behind. Millions of dollars have been allocated from our grants and contracts to help others. Now, we are faced with an increasing community need and there are no funds to meet this escalating crisis of juveniles on our streets. We want to hire a counselor; however, a 13-week aftercare counseling pilot program costs $13,000. Can you help? I'm enclosing a prestamped envelope for your use. Hurry, it's not getting any safer on our streets!

- Remember the famous song by John Denver, "Take Me Home, Country Roads"? Well, you already know that our country roads are killing our first responder vehicles, year by year, dollar after dollar for wear and tear–related maintenance. Every fire alarm creates multiple internal alarms for our volunteers. The Friends of the Bostwick Fire Department have a solution to the Department's needs. If we can identify 10 to 15 new friends—from our community—willing to contribute financially to our equipment fund—we can present the Department with a new pumper truck before 2013 rolls around. I know you're wondering what happened to our need for turnout gear. Well, last week, Edna Myers walked into the station and gave us a check for $15,000 (raised from church bake sales) to purchase new gear. We need you!

CHAPTER 6

The Closing

This final chapter in Part One gives you the three final steps to closing your fundraising letter or e-mail. First, I'll give you compelling closing lines. Second, I'll show you some signature art (traditional signatures with request-related artwork). Finally, we'll close this chapter with impacting postscripts.

Few fundraisers really spend time writing the closing to their letters. Most have a standard closing like the historically boring *sincerely yours*. It's time to have a little fun and think outside of the box.

Elements of the Closing

1. Write a Compelling Closing Line.

2. The Art of Your Signature.

3. The Impacting Postscript.

1. Write a Compelling Closing Line

Most of us use standard closing templates in all of our letters, from fundraising to other types of business letters. The closing line is not something we've spent much time on because we have assumed that there's not a lot to do in one simple final line. Wrong! The closing line must be linked to your entire letter's theme. It's cleverly creative. I don't know of any other way to describe the closing line. When I'm writing my funding request letters, I spend at least 30 minutes brainstorming perfect phrases for *eye candy* closings. (As in the past chapters in Part One, I am closing out this section by picking up on the same 12 agencies profiled in Chapters 1 through 5. This way, you can see the complete letter for each organization by simply perusing Chapters 1 through 6 anytime.)

Here are the perfect phrases for compelling closing lines. (Remember, each line ends with a comma because this is the last line before your signature line.)

- Concerned about the health of our children,
- Making a difference—one child at a time,
- Saving the wetlands for future generations,
- Helping Vale attract art patrons,
- Saving Sunset's youngest stakeholders,
- Smiles, laughs, and a diagnosis,

- Educating, informing, and entertaining,
- Maintaining the rhythm of life on our campus,
- Maslow's hierarchy of needs included children,
- Bringing our troops home to a home,
- Aftercare—the only answer to safe streets,
- Gathering community to rally around the department's needs,

2. The Art of Your Signature

I know that you're wondering how you can beef up your standard signature in fundraising letters. Well, I think that your signature line can be a combination of artwork and your standard signature. In these examples, here's the order of information and artwork:

1. Signature line
2. Artwork
3. Signatory's title
4. Name of asking organization

This is like adding your own personal seal of uniqueness.

Figure 6-1 shows some art-inspired signature lines.

Figure 6-1 Art-Inspired Signature Lines

Lacey Ruggles, Ed.D.

Principal
St. Matthews Elementary
School

Source: Used with permission
from http://www.fotosearch
.com/illustration/asthma.html.

David Wyman, Jr., CFRE

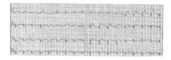

Development Director
Kansas State University Foundation

Source: http://en.wikipedia.org/wiki/
File:12_Lead_EKG_ST_Elevation
_tracing_only.jpg

Retired Col. Adolph Klinker

Volunteer Director
The Home Soon Promise

Source: http://en.wikipedia.org/wiki/
File:Southern_California.png

Cliff Abrahamson, GPC, CFRE, AFP

Fund Development Director
Tucson Chapter—Big Brothers
Big Sisters of America

Source: http://www
.tucsonbigs.org/

Altsoba Yazzi, AFP

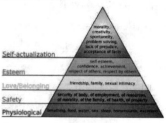

Development Director
Navajo Nation School District

Source: http://en.wikipedia.org/wiki/
File:Maslow%27s_hierarchy_of
_needs.svg

Mel Jackson

Founder and Executive Director
Leadership Training Institute

Source: http://no.wikipedia.org/wiki/
Fil:Working_Together_Teamwork
_Puzzle_Concept.jpg

3. The Impacting Postscript

This is the last line in your fundraising letters and e-mails. It's a postscript, abbreviated P.S., and it's added after the main body of the letter or e-mail. The term comes from the Latin *post scriptum*, an expression meaning "written after" (which may be interpreted in the sense of "that which comes after the writing"). A postscript may be a sentence, a paragraph, or occasionally many paragraphs added, often hastily and incidentally, after the signature of a letter.

Let's get started on some perfect phrases for this final leg of your letter! (I'm going to use the same 12 organizations that I've been profiling in the examples found in Chapters 1 through 5.) Remember, this is the final typed line in your letters. Use italics to write your P.S.

- *Robert, once a St. Matt student, always a St. Matt student. You'll always be one of our most successful alumni!*

- *Sharon, I want to extend an invitation to you to volunteer with our program. We'd be delighted to have you join your sister-in-law as one of our valuable volunteers.*

- *Jeff, you can start your family's legacy with this first environment-saving action. You can make so many memories to pass on to your children and their heirs as well...*

- *Emily, sometimes in our lives we really want to do something that makes a difference. It's our footprint or legacy for everyone who comes after us.*

- *Andrew, I think Marion Wright Edelman said it best: "If we don't stand up for children, then we don't stand for much." Let's stand up for the kids living on the streets near your neighborhood!*

- *Mildred, I found this quote about a person with Angelman syndrome: "I may not speak, but I have a lot to say." Words to remember and learn from…*

- *Jeremy, ensuring the future of our public airwaves and preserving quality programming for children should be a mission that all embrace…*

- *Carol, on a final note, I wanted to convey my sympathy for the loss of your Jim. I read in the paper that he had a heart attack while working on our campus. Perhaps, we can talk about a way to memorialize Jim throughout the campus…*

- *Marcus, I want to share this quote with you: "I guess I so desperately want to see us put this planet right. It's so horrifying to me that a fifth of us are starving every night, and that forty thousand children die every single day." I believe that ultimately we are all responsible for feeding America's children.*

- *Capt. Mathers, caring for our veterans is the duty of a grateful nation.*

- *Judy, financing aftercare programs for juvenile offenders is no longer a government priority; we must step up as a community to assure that these youth receive critically needed services.*

- *Honorable Judge Richardson, firefighters are indispensable foot soldiers here at home.*

PART II

PERFECT PHRASES FOR INTERNET AND SOCIAL MEDIA CAMPAIGNS

CHAPTER 7

Organization Website Campaigns

The Internet has made it possible for every type of fundraising campaign to be made public to the entire world. The first stop on the World Wide Web is ramping up your organization's website for a fundraising campaign. Before we get started with perfect phrases for organization website campaigns, let's explore what it takes to make your website a search engine and hit (someone clicking on your website address) magnet.

First, choose a website name that is easy for potential contributors to find on the Internet. Typically, smaller grassroots nonprofit organizations choose websites that have convoluted long names that only they can remember—for example, www .helpnetvolunteers@godaddy.com/helpnet. This is way too long! How about shortening it to www.helpnet.org?

Second, design your website for easy readability. Don't have too many tabs, and most important, make sure you have tabs for *About Us*, *Contact Us*, *Donate*, and *Who Does Your Donation*

Help or *How Does Your Contribution Make a Difference*. Those are the only tabs that potential contributors look for. The *About Us* tab should give information on your organization, its Board of Directors, staff, programs, and partners. Here are some good examples of *About Us* web pages for you to check out online:

- National Council of Nonprofits—http://www.councilof nonprofits.org/who-we-are
- Association of American Fundraising Professionals— http://www.afpnet.org/about/?navItemNumber=500
- Certified Fundraising Executives International—http:// www.cfre.org/about.html

The *Contact Us* tab should not just be a fill-in box. Contact Us should provide a street address, telephone and fax numbers, e-mail addresses for key staff (Executive Director and Development Director at a minimum), and your operating hours. Make sure to include a link to map software for potential contributors needing directions to your location. Here are some good examples of *Contact Us* web pages to check out online:

- Nonprofit Finance Fund—http://nonprofitfinancefund .org/contact-us
- The Nonprofit Association of Oregon—http://www.non profitoregon.org/about_us/contact_us
- Genesis Non-Profit Housing Corporation—http://www .genesisnphc.org/contact_us.htm

The *Donate* tab should be linked to an automated shopping cart. Some very good examples of online *Donate* options can be viewed on these websites:

- March of Dimes—http://www.marchofdimes.com/giving/ giving.html

- American Cancer Society—https://www.cancer.org/ involved/donate/donateonlinenow/index

- American Red Cross—http://www.redcross.org/donate/ donate.html

The *Who Does Your Donation Help* or *How Does Your Contribution Make a Difference* tab is where we develop perfect phrases content to fuel our website fundraising campaigns. In this chapter, I give you examples of how to create appeal magnetism that steers potential contributors to hit the *Donate* link or tab as soon as they read your compelling *Who Does Your Donation Help* tab's content. Some very good examples of *Who Does Your Donation Help* or *How Does Your Contribution Make a Difference* tabs can be viewed on these websites:

- Stop Abuse for Everyone—http://www.safe4all.org/ donate/

- Children of Bali—http://childrenofbali.org/make-a -donation/how-will-my-donations-help/

- Goodwill Industries International, Inc.—http://www.good will.org/get-involved/donate/

The remainder of the chapter gives examples of perfect phrases for this key element of organization website campaigns, the *Who Does Your Donation Help* or *How Does Your Contribution Make a Difference?* tab.

Who Does Your Donation Help or How Does Our Organization Make a Difference?

Potential contributors not only want to know about the appealing organization, they also want to know how their money will be used or who their contribution will help move from a dire situation to a more desirable situation. When you are designing content for the *Who Does Your Donation Help* or *How Does Our Organization Make a Difference* web page, it's important to include a list of significant differences that will occur as a result of the donations. For example, if you're raising funds for iPads for every student in your K–5 elementary school, don't focus on the needed technology. Your primary focus should be on the young children who do not have access to any technology outside of their classrooms along with research on the impact of using iPads in classrooms. If you use names of individuals, remember to change the actual name of the individuals, and don't include any photos or videos without signed parent and/or guardian permission forms.

Here are some examples for perfect phrases for *Who Does Your Donation Help*. Remember, this web page is very similar to a statement of need or description of the problem in a fundraising letter campaign.

- Your contribution will enable the Fort McDowall Animal Welfare Society to:
  - ❖ Provide care packages for animals living with low-income families.
  - ❖ Continue the Adopt-a-Pet program on the first Saturday of every month.
  - ❖ Cover expenses for veterinarian fees, new collars, flea dips, and neutering/spaying. Because of you, cash-strapped families will be able to adopt a pet for $10 rather than our usual fee of $100.

- An investment of $250 in Walnut Tree Arts and Cultural Center will help:
  - ❖ Children like Sammie and Sarah, whose foster family cannot afford Summer Cultural Camp.
  - ❖ Struggling artists like Elmer, who lived in the alley behind the Center. Elmer was discovered when one of our staff members saw his paintings on adjacent cement block fences. She found Elmer painting his heart out with discarded cans of old house paint. The mural became a community bonding centerpiece for *Taking Back Our Streets*. We hired Elmer to do part-time custodial work at the Center in exchange for providing his art supplies and giving him shared studio time to paint on canvas. His works are revolutionary because he is painting the community from the eyes of a homeless person. With contributions, the Center will purchase frames and hold a gallery viewing for Elmer. All funds will be managed by his guardian (we

found a long-lost relative to help him get off of the streets).

● The YWCA of Greater Rockland critically needs your donation in order to:

❖ Expand our residential capacity from 40 rooms to 50 rooms. The additional rooms will accommodate 10 single female victims of domestic violence who have a home and will transition out of the shelter in 90 days. A donation of $1,500 will allow us to convert a meeting room into four two-person living units. Walls and doors will be added and basic furnishings will be purchased.

● A donation of $5,000 will enable the First Nations Economic Development Corporation to reinvest in some of the microenterprise business plans currently under review by our Grant Committee:

❖ Eddie Wildflower has a new concept for recycling. It will reduce waste at landfills by 50 percent and increase the landfill's life cycle by 10 years. Development phase cost: $1,000.

❖ Ramona Moon Rising plans to create a native language DVD set to teach native children the Seven Generations philosophy of life. This series will be produced, duplicated, and distributed by disabled elders on the Seminole Reservation. Cost: $1,500.

❖ The Amitola family (Dad, Mom, and four adult children) want to open an auto repair business on the borders of South and North Dakota. The nearest auto repair

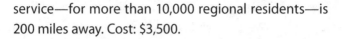

service—for more than 10,000 regional residents—is 200 miles away. Cost: $3,500.

● The Davidson One-Stop Career Center provides client support services that are not covered by our federal and state grants from the Department of Labor. Your contribution will fulfill the following wish lists:

❖ $50 will purchase 30 days of mass transportation passes for a client who just started a new job after 13 years of chronic unemployment. Her first payday is 30 days from the date of hire.

❖ $100 will purchase one professional business suit for a client that needs to be dressed in appropriate clothing for a series of job interviews.

❖ $150 will purchase nursing shoes for a client ready to start her practicum in nursing at a local hospital.

❖ $200 will purchase a refurbished netbook computer for a client that is attending college (a first for her family in three generations) and needs to write school papers. She is holding two part-time jobs and is the mother of four young children. The college's computer lab is not open when she works on her papers in the middle of the night.

● The Midwest Disability Center has five new clients from Lechia. These are our most pressing needs where your contribution will be allocated:

❖ $4,500 will purchase an electronic standing wheelchair for a paraplegic client that migrated to the United

States and has no financial resources or healthcare coverage. With this wheelchair, the client will be able to participate in sheltered workshop classes and learn a trade.

❖ $5,000 will purchase 10 talking business calculators for 10 of our visually impaired clients that are enrolled in a business accounting class.

❖ $6,000 will purchase 30 personal listeners with neck loops for our hard of hearing clients. These devices are configured for up to 60 decibels amplification with maximum volume gain and bass reduction controls.

● HIV/AIDS prevention outreach at Caring Bridges Social Services Agency is making a difference. Your contributions will help us carry out community education forums targeting high-risk individuals and urge them to seek testing and treatment. Here's how you can help us:

❖ $50 will print 100 color educational posters for distribution in locales frequented by high-risk individuals.

❖ $100 will pay an honorarium to a HIV/AIDS speaker.

❖ $200 will pay for two hours of disease prevention counseling.

❖ $400 will pay for four doses of medication for a client with no healthcare insurance and not eligible for public assistance coverage.

❖ $800 will sponsor a community forum (four hours of education and awareness presentations and small group discussions about the increasing prevalence of HIV/AIDS in our community).

● The Civitan Foundation of Southern Nevada and Arizona urgently needs your sponsorship for the 2013 summer camp season. Every $250 received sends one disabled child or young adult to Camp Civitan, located in Williams, Arizona.

❖ $250 sends one eager and excited inner-city camper to our program.

❖ $500 sends two excited campers to Williams.

❖ $1,000 sends four wait-list campers for two weeks of recreation and bonding.

❖ $2,000 sends and transports eight campers to our remote year-round location.

❖ $4,000 sponsors an entire camp group (varying ages) of 16 ready-to-pack campers!

● When Ophelia Bonner died, we promised to carry on her tradition of awarding two community college scholarships each spring to students from our rural and remote high school. Your contribution to the Ophelia Bonner Scholarship Fund can help one or both of this year's candidates to start their higher education journey. Here's the breakdown of how every dollar donated can help:

❖ _____ Yes, I want to contribute $250 to buy textbooks for one semester.

❖ _____ Yes, I want to contribute $500 to buy textbooks for two semesters.

❖ _____ Yes, I want to contribute $1,650 to pay one semester of tuition for a full-time student.

❖ _____ Yes, I want to contribute $3,300 to pay for two semesters of tuition for a full-time student.

❖ _____ Yes, I can contribute $_____ to be applied toward education expenses.

Note: It's okay to have open options or a dropdown box where contributors can select other items rather than a limited set list.

● St. Morgan's Church is launching a fundraising campaign to build a new building. We've set up a pretty nifty formula on a per-brick sponsorship price. Please help us build our bricks (and mortar) and get this building started and finished in the next year!

❖ $1,000 buys one brick with your family's last name on a small bronze-plated plaque.

❖ $2,000 buys two bricks with the first name of two family members on a silver-plated plaque.

❖ $4,000 buys four bricks with the first and last names of four family members on a gold-plated plaque.

● The Northlands Community Food Bank needs your contribution TODAY! Every dollar donated will go toward providing food boxes to needy individuals and families.

❖ $25 buys a week's worth of fresh fruit and includes a $5 coupon for fresh produce at a local food cooperative.

❖ $50 buys a week's worth of boxed and canned goods and vegetables for a family of four.

❖ $100 buys a week's worth of meal supplies for a family of eight.

❖ Every dollar feeds a stomach that is often empty and warms a heart that is often hard because being hungry is a hard situation to be in when you're a parent and your children look to you for the basics. Please help us to help our clients!

● Soccer for Everyone, International is suffering financially from this world recession. How can you help? By donating to our organization and helping us to keep promoting and sponsoring international soccer events for youth, ages 7 to 17 years old. Approximately 100 events per year have been requested; however, funds are scarce. Please help us meet these requests.

❖ €74.75 euros ($100 U.S.) will pay for one refereed event.

❖ €373.77 euros ($500 U.S.) will pay for five refereed events.

❖ €747.5 euros ($1,000 U.S.) will pay for 10 refereed events.

● The Latino Social Club of Boise is raising funds for a new building. We are asking you to sponsor a room. Please consider forming a group of 10 or more members and planning some small fundraising events to raise the minimum needed to sponsor a room. We really need your help. We are asking for advance pledges (via our website) so we know that you can be counted on to make your contribution by December 31, 2013. Please look at the purpose for each room and select your favorite room early. Thanks!

❖ The Gathering Room will be used for meetings where 25 to 50 persons will need to be accommodated. It will be 1,500 square feet and state of the art for furnishings, meeting presentation technology, and soundproofing. $25,000 sponsor needed.

❖ Handicapped-accessible restrooms (four) are needed to accommodate large groups. Energy-efficient fixtures will be installed to reduce water and electricity use (lowering the cost to maintain our new building). $50,000 sponsor needed.

❖ Mama's Kitchen will be our commercial food preparation space. This will be a separate nonprofit enterprise that will be used to train our youth how to purchase food, prepare gourmet meals, and properly serve visitors using our space including our own members. $75,000 sponsor needed.

● *Remember, all sponsors have 24 months to raise 100 percent of funding for the selected room(s). Submit your commitment online today, and one of our Board members will contact you with specifics and to share our blueprints with you and your fundraising team.*

CHAPTER 8

YouTube Campaigns

With YouTube, your fundraising campaigns can come to life in video format. This sounds and looks easy when we view the existing fundraising videos on YouTube. However, this polished presentation takes a lot of planning. Before you can get started, it's critical to develop a story script.

This chapter will focus on the elements of a story script and give you examples of some perfect phrases for story scripts.

Elements of YouTube Campaigns

1. Point of View.

2. Dramatic Question.

3. Emotional Content.

Source: www.techsoup.org/learningcenter/training/page6738
.cfm

1. Point of View

Before you can tell your organization's story, you must think about what's important to share with your YouTube viewers and what's not. The best way to get started is to ask yourself what is the message we are trying to send out, why is it important to share this message, and who is the target for our message? Will you tell your story from the organization's point of view or the client's point of view? You get started with a lead line. These ear-catching and attention-getting lines can range from one to six appeal-starting statements spoken at the beginning of your YouTube video.

Here are some perfect phrases for point-of-view lead lines.

- **Animal and Wildlife Fundraising**
  - ❖ Organization view: The Sitka Wildlife Rescue Foundation is running out of funds, and the wildlife that we can't rescue will succumb to man's destructive patterns.
  - ❖ Client view: Just yesterday, Harvey, an oil-covered walrus, looked on with concern as the Sitka Wildlife Rescue Foundation's team rescue team tried to save Harvey's slowly suffocating offspring—who were not as lucky as Harvey was.

- **Arts and Culture Fundraising**
  - ❖ Organization view: Ballet Moscow's production costs have exceeded our ticket revenues and contributions 3:1 for the past two years.

❖ Client view: An audience member at one of our ballet performances recently came backstage at Ballet Moscow and made this devastating comment: "What happened to the people who used to come and enjoy the ballet? The seats were full, now there are more empty seats than full ones.

● **Children and Families Fundraising**

❖ Organization view: Jordan Lane Foster Care can't last three more months without your contributions.

❖ Client view: Michael, Jamie, and Cathy Ann didn't ask to be placed in foster care. Their lives were changed overnight when both of their parents were arrested for drug possession. The cost to care for them at Jordan Lane Foster Care is $1,500 monthly. The state only pays for $600 of their foster care expenses. They have no place else to go.

● **Community and Economic Development Fundraising**

❖ Organization view: The Christmas Community Development Corporation is faced with its greatest financial challenge. Our funding has not been renewed by the state of Michigan, and we're in dire straits when it comes to having the critically needed financial resources to bring new businesses and dollars into our small community.

❖ Client view: Jerry's business expansion loan was approved by the Christmas Community Development Corporation six months ago. Yet today, Jerry still does not have the $25,000 he was counting on to purchase another mobile dog grooming van for his growing business. He is cash strapped and wondering how he will end the year without being in the red financially.

- **Computers and Technology Fundraising**
  - ❖ Organization view: The Street Front Learning Lab promises our students state of the art technology; yet, in all reality, we have not been able to update our computers in six years.
  - ❖ Client view: Muriel and 30 other low-income clients enrolled at the Street Front Learning Lab in hopes of starting their filmmaking careers. She and the other students are so disappointed that our outdated computers cannot run the current moviemaking software. They shouldn't be punished for our financial difficulties.

- **Disability Fundraising**
  - ❖ Organization view: Jacob's Sheltered Workshop is running out of materials and supplies for its 75 physically and mentally challenged students. Our students have been making widgets for local businesses for seven years. The revenue that comes in helps to purchase additional materials and supplies. With the economic downturn, many of our business clients have closed or cut back. The fate of our program is in your hands.
  - ❖ Client view: Myron is 26 years old and severely mentally impaired. He eagerly looks forward to attending Jacob's Sheltered Workshop three days a week. For

Myron, it means that he won't be sitting in front of a television until his caregiver has some free time. He also misses the weekly allowance he has been earning. Myron is saving up for his own shaving kit—one he doesn't have to share with the other residents at his residential living facility. Most of all, he misses the business owners that he interacted with when his widgets passed the buyer's rigorous inspections.

● **Education and Literacy Fundraising**
  ❖ Organization view: The Youngstown Literacy Council has been in its current building for 23 years. Today, we found out that our landlord has let the building go into foreclosure. With little notice, we are faced with having to find new offices and client/student meeting rooms. There is no way to prepare for the upcoming costs of a rental deposit, moving expenses, and likely higher monthly rent.
  ❖ Client view: Margaret is 64 years old and could not read when she came to the Youngstown Literacy Council for help. She wanted to file for social security when she turned 62, but she was too embarrassed to ask for help to fill out the forms. Margaret is probably eligible for disability, but she has had to take in other people's laundry for the past 10 years in order to eat and pay rent.

● **Environment and Conservation Fundraising**
  ❖ Organization view: The ECOLIFE Foundation needs your help in reducing the deforestation of the trees on

which the monarch butterflies depend. This escalating problem is caused by forest fires and the resulting massive smoke caused by inefficient woodburning stoves that are being used for cooking and eating by people living around the butterfly sanctuaries.

❖ Client view: When Maria gathered the wood for her family, she did not know that the antiquated wood stove would overheat and burn 200 acres adjacent to the Monarch Butterfly Sanctuary. The ECOLIFE Foundation exploration team found the burned-out acreage on our last educational mission to Maria's homeland. For both the butterflies that did not return because of the smoke and Maria's village, the loss is immeasurable.

● **HIV/AIDS Prevention Fundraising**

❖ Organization view: The Minority AIDS Coalition is facing its greatest challenge. Seven of our clients are in a crisis stage. Their incomes have been cut off by their inability to work. The cost of their life-lengthening medication has not been covered by the state for six months. Our client support services fund is as bare as Old Mother Hubbard's cupboard. Many of these medications cost as much as $100 per dose. The Coalition is between a rock and a hard place.

❖ Client view: Edgar is 60 years old. He's was diagnosed with HIV 20 years ago. For the past two decades, earnings from his part-time job have helped him pay for critically needed medications. Edgar, along with seven other Minority AIDS Coalition clients, is at a life bridge that they can't cross without your help. Their life-lengthening medications are costing upwards of $100 each per dose. Clients like Edgar take two or three pills per day. For the past few months since Edgar and his friends have been laid off, they have had to make a choice about which pill to take and which one to save for another day. This is America, and this shouldn't be happening. We should not have to make a choice between partial lifesaving and no lifesaving!

- **Hunger and Homeless Fundraising**
  - ❖ Organization view: The Valley of the Sun Food Bank is running out of food. I know this may be hard to believe, but our food donations from local grocery stores and food cooperatives have dropped in the past three months. We used to be able to give an individual or a family one box of fruit, one bag of vegetables, and one carton of dry goods. Lately, it's been a choice of one of the three food pyramid items. Sadly, we don't know where to turn in order to restock our shelves. This means actually having to purchase food staples at retail prices. Taking this approach means that a year's worth of operating funds will be used up in about four months!
  - ❖ Client view: Miguel is married to Lizbetta, and together they have nine children. They used to have a home (before foreclosure), and both parents worked hard to provide food and shelter for their children. Last year, Miguel was hurt on his construction job and he is now wheelchair bound. Lizbetta lost her part-time job as church secretary when attendance declined. They are

struggling to get by on their unemployment and disability checks. Foreclosure took place recently, and they are now staying with family.

● **International Rescue Fundraising**

❖ Organization view: Divers Rescue International members have been called on 850 times in the past year. From New Zealand to Guam to Japan, our services have been in high demand. Unfortunately, the cost of rescue missions has been greater than incoming contributions. It's the end of the year, and it may be the end of Divers Rescue International volunteer disaster relief efforts.

❖ Client view: When the earthquakes and resulting tsunami hit the coast of Japan, many elders could not swim or outrun these back-to-back flooding disasters. More than 2,000 families were lost on the exterior islands. One of those families represented four generations, from a 95-year-old great-grandfather, Asa, to a four-month-old infant, Miyoki. As the head of his village, Asa was a strong and faithful community leader. In the blink of an eye, everything and everyone was gone.

● **Faith-Based Fundraising**

❖ Organization view: Christian Counseling Associates cannot bill third-party insurance companies for our services. Regretfully, we are not an eligible provider because of our faith-based approach to counseling young children that are victims of abuse. Last year, we served 500 children under a subcontract with the local courts. Our compensation was $25 per child. One hour of intensive counseling costs us $125.

❖ Client view: Ella was seven years old when her aunt broke her arm after she accidentally knocked a glass vase off of the shelf. She was nine years old when she suffered second-degree burns from someone in her family throwing boiling water on her. Once she was removed from this abusive situation, her foster parents brought her to Christian Counseling Associates. Their ability to pay $125 per hour was hampered by the actual amount that the state will reimburse them ($45 per hour). We didn't turn Ella away. She still received 60 hours of intensive counseling made available by donors like you.

● **Scholarship Fundraising**

❖ Organization view: Mott Community College Foundation has desperately been trying to raise funds for the Sherman Mitchell Scholarship Fund. Started in 2000, this fund has helped over 20 students study music at our college. Many of these students did not have a way to pay tuition and were not eligible for a Pell grant. To take out a student loan would result in a financial burden for our students and their working poor families.

❖ Client view: Shelly, a music student at Mott Community College, plays a mean sax. (Note to reader: Shelly is playing her saxophone music in the background.) She dreamed for years about attending college and getting a degree in music education and performing arts. With many barriers in the way, Shelly came to our financial aid office in tears.

● **Law Enforcement Fundraising**

❖ Organization view: The City of Camden's Police Department has been in such dire financial straits that our officer's spouses formed a Friends of Camden Police Department Foundation. Working and already overextended spouses are now trying to plan and hold fundraisers in order to come up with the funding needed to restore three full-time positions that were eliminated when property tax revenues dropped (our foreclosure rate hit 73 percent).

❖ Client view: My husband, Brian, is a 20-year veteran with the City of Camden's Police Department. Every day, his life is at risk in order to make our community safe. Last year, three of Brian's coworkers (with young children like ours) were laid off permanently. The City's revenues have simply tanked due to a high number of foreclosures and the bankruptcy filed by our 50-year-old lumber mill. Brian puts in a lot of unpaid overtime because of the labor shortage. I gathered a group of officers' spouses and we formed the Friends of Camden Police Department Foundation. It's time to roll up our sleeves and help this community!

● **Sports-Related Fundraising**

❖ Organization view: The Little League Baseball Foundation is going to have to shut its doors in six months. What happened? Our contributions simply dried up.

We have struggled to support, sponsor, and grow League baseball throughout a 26-county region for 29 years. It's too bad that the really good things must come to a fateful end and our world's bad influences seem to last forever.

❖ Client view: The Kelley triplets played Little League baseball with the help of the Little League Baseball Foundation for the first 13 years of their life. Today, the Kelly triplets are all signed with Major League Baseball teams and giving back to their community. However, financial difficulties for the Little League Baseball Foundation cannot be solved with donations from one family.

● **Health-Related Fundraising**

❖ Organization view: The Foss Avenue Assisted Living Center is struggling with ever-increasing winter heating expenses. With inadequate insulation coupled with a 90-year-old facility and non-energy-efficient windows, our natural gas bills have been upwards of $7,000 a month since November 12 when local temperatures dropped below freezing 45 days earlier than in past years.

❖ Client view: Ella and Mac, married 60 years, have been residents at Foss Avenue Assisted Living Center for the past six years. When they celebrated their 60th wedding anniversary at our facility last month, they had to ask their 140 guests to keep their coats on. It was 10 below zero that day, and we simply could not turn up our thermostats for fear of another $7,000+ natural gas bill. Keeping the thermostat down on a daily basis means that residents like Ella and Mac are cold 24 hours a day, seven days a week.

2. Dramatic Question

Once you've written your lead line, it's important to incorporate one dramatic question. You pose this question to crate compassion among your YouTube audience. This is not an actual question that you expect anyone to answer; it's a rhetorical question that forces the viewer to think about the situation.

Here are some perfect phrases for dramatic questions.

- **Animal and Wildlife Fundraising**
  Can you imagine the pain related to Harvey's loss?

- **Arts and Culture Fundraising**
  How will Ballet Moscow survive without event marketing dollars?

- **Children and Families Fundraising**
  If Jordan Lane can't afford to care for Michael, Jamie, and Cathy Ann, where will they go?

- **Community and Economic Development Fundraising**
  Did you know that it takes dollars to make dollars?

- **Computers and Technology Fundraising**
  Do you remember the old Radio Shack TRS-80 computers (circa 1990) and how antiquated they would be today?

- **Disability Fundraising**
  Do you know what it feels like to look at the disappointment on Myron's face?

- **Education and Literacy Fundraising**
  Eviction is nearing—how did it come to this?

- **Environment and Conservation Fundraising**
  What will happen when the Monarch Butterfly Sanctuary no longer exists?

- **HIV/AIDS Prevention Fundraising**
  How long will our clients have to choose which one of their life-lengthening pills they will take?

- **Hunger and Homeless Fundraising**
  Do we just turn off the lights and put out a sign that our shelves are empty?

- **International Rescue Fundraising**
  Who's going to dive for the bodies in the next water-related world disaster?

- **Faith-Based Fundraising**
  Atheists have been slowly taking the Christ out of everything. Is counseling next?

- **Scholarship Fundraising**
  Can you imagine if all of today's top musicians weren't given a chance?

- **Law Enforcement Fundraising**
  Can you imagine if Brian and his colleagues were so tired that they made a fatal mistake, one that caused injury or death in their department?

- **Sports-Related Fundraising**
  Did you know that Little League Baseball Foundation is no one's priority except ours and yours?

- **Health-Related Fundraising**
  Do you know that for the residents in assisted living this is their last stop before the graveyard?

3. Emotional Content

Language that includes incidences of loss, redemption, crisis, or change is key to keeping your audience engaged and interested. Emotional content is a common denominator that everyone can relate to, and it's what makes your fundraising appeals so universally magnetizing.

Here are some perfect phrases for emotional content.

- **Animal and Wildlife Fundraising**
  The Sitka Wildlife Rescue Foundation is operating in crisis mode! We need your contributions to keep the doors open. Every dollar will make a difference for Harvey and other rescued wildlife. Please donate on our website: www.helpharvey.org.

- **Arts and Culture Fundraising**
  Thousands of community members have never heard of Ballet Moscow. Because we do not have the funds for marketing outreach, our sales are limited to past patrons and people who stumble upon our website or box office by

accident. You can change our future by donating today at www.balletmoscow.net.

● **Children and Families Fundraising**
These children have victimized all of their lives by adults that they trusted. Now, with funding drying up for extra foster care expenses, they are being victimized by the system designed to protect and shelter them. You can help these siblings stay at Jordan Lane Foster Care by contributing at www.jordanlanecare.net.

● **Community and Economic Development Fundraising**
When businesses need to expand in order to increase their customer base and revenues and no loans are available, eventually, the business will be suffocated financially. It will only take a few suffocated and closed businesses to kill a community economically. Please help to keep our community alive and economically thriving. Donate at www.christmasalive.org.

● **Computers and Technology Fundraising**
Without updated computer technology, Muriel and her classmates will have to learn the filmmaking process by watching canned videos on YouTube. There will be no hands-on learning on our antiquated low-memory and low-megahertz computers! This is an urgent situation! Please contribute to our equipment fund at www.street front.net.

● **Disability Fundraising**
Jacob's Sheltered Workshop is the only means of income for 75 special needs adults. The chances of our students

finding similar paying work in the public sector are slim or next to nothing. Jacob's is their home, their day life, and their means of income. Please donate at www.jacobs place.org.

● **Education and Literacy Fundraising**

Volunteer literacy services are a critically needed community service. There are still hundreds of parents and grandparents in our community who have hidden the fact that they can't read for years. When they finally rally the courage to come forward and ask for help, we're not going to have a location to offer that help in.... Please donate at www.volunteerlit.org.

● **Environment and Conservation Fundraising**

Human beings have knowingly and unknowingly destroyed life-form sanctuaries worldwide. Providing safer woodburning stoves for adjacent villages in Mexico makes a lot of sense and COSTS A LOT OF CENTS! Help change a century-old way of cooking by donating to www.savethe sanctuarynow.org.

● **HIV/AIDS Prevention Fundraising**

Edgar and other clients like him cannot live much longer without following their physician-prescribed medications on a daily basis—every day! You can help by supporting our client support services fund. Edgar is hopeful that you'll donate at www.macforlife.org.

● **Hunger and Homeless Fundraising**

Many agencies, individuals, and families depend on our food bank. All of the magic tricks and miracles we pulled off in the past are no longer working. Help! Please donate now to www.vsfb.org.

- **International Rescue Fundraising**

   We are a volunteer diving rescue organization. Many of our members must take unpaid leave from work to assist with world water-related disasters. Another airplane could plunge into the ocean or even the New York harbor. We have to be prepared, and that means having the money to pay for search and rescue efforts. Can you please help us by donating at www.dri.net?

- **Faith-Based Fundraising**

   Our specialty is providing Christ-centered counseling to abused children. If we can't keep our doors open or we have to turn these children away, it would be a sad and horrible decision. We don't want to have to make this decision. Your donation can help. Please donate at www.cca.net.

- **Scholarship Fundraising**

   Sherman Mitchell (the scholarship is named after him) is 82 years old. He is a jazz legacy, and he has donated his time to perform at fundraising concerts for 12 years. The bulk of our scholarship funds are derived from his contribution. Unfortunately, Sherman is in stage 4 of leukemia and he can no longer perform at our fundraisers. This is going to put a major damper on attendance when it's not going to be Sherman. Can you help us keep this fund going? Can you donate today at www.mccf.org?

● **Law Enforcement Fundraising**
Our City is under state receivership. This means that all monies that were managed by the city are now being managed by the state. There is a freeze on all payroll, overtime has been eliminated (although overtime hours have gone unpaid for what seems like forever), and times are looking dire for our police department. We urgently need your help. Please donate to our fund so that we can help the city and the state bring back at least one foot patrol officer under private sector sponsorship. Today! Please donate at fcpdf.org.

● **Sports-Related Fundraising**
The role models for our kids are not on television, they're here on the fields. Our barely paid referees and other caring adults need a morale boost. The lack of funds is killing the spirits and hopes of children, their families, and our dedicated team members. We need your help today! Please contribute today to continue our efforts to keep the Foundation's mission in action. Donate in www.llbf.

● **Health-Related Fundraising**
We have started a utility fund. In order to keep up with current bills and pay the monies in arrear ($37,000), we desperately need your help! Please donate to www.faalc.org.

CHAPTER 9

Facebook Campaigns

With Facebook fundraising campaigns, you must focus on creating *read me* media content within their affiliated Causes (www.causes.com) application. This application is a valuable tool for nonprofit organizations. It allows charities to promote their cause and build communities through Facebook's social networking capabilities. In the same way that users join groups, they can also join a cause. Anyone can set up a cause for your organization and use his or her network on Facebook to raise awareness and run advocacy programs for your organization.

Once you have created a cause, the next thing to do is to gain supporters. Because you are the moderator of your cause, you are in control of all aspects of its appearance. Users will not see your profile or your nonprofit page through your cause (though you can link to them if you wish).

You can invite those in your contact list to support your cause, or you can wait and hope that people will find your cause when they are searching through Facebook. Another good way to market your cause is to write notes with the note application and post them on your personal profile page and your nonprofit page.

Pictures, quotes, videos, links to other sites—use as many "marketing" tricks as you can to promote your cause. You can only have one picture; however, you can have photo albums on other sites that you can link to. As well, remember that a cause doesn't have to necessarily reflect your organization's overall goal. You can set up a cause to promote an upcoming event or program, or to simply increase awareness of your organization's profile. But remember: make sure your cause has a functional link to your organization's home page!

Source: http://mycharityconnects.org

This chapter will focus on magnetizing examples of perfect phrases content for your Facebook Causes page.

Elements of Facebook Campaigns

1. Create a Compelling Impact-Based Fundraising Campaign.
2. Send Regular Brief Updates About the Campaign.

1. Create a Compelling Impact-Based Fundraising Campaign

Rather than just creating new language for this section of Chapter 9, I spent a full day scrolling through facebook.com/causes looking for examples of perfect phrases that leaped off of the computer screen and called my name to GIVE. The common characteristics of these Facebook Causes appeals are the short to lengthy *read more about us* lead lines and paragraphs.

You can find tons of fundraising campaign messages at facebook.com/causes; when you click through, you will land on the causes.com web page. Remember, Causes is a mini-application linked to Facebook, but it is not owned by Facebook. Most of the examples that I found on causes.com had videos (YouTube links) to show their target population or discuss their causes' purpose and request a donation.

Here are the best examples (Dr. Bev's favorites) of perfect phrases to replicate for your Facebook Causes fundraising campaign. I have **bolded** the words and phrases that really grab potential donors' attention.

- Check out the Dallas Cowboys' Wish for the Salvation Army—they are well on their way to $50,000 but **they need your help**. Make a donation today at this link and be entered to win some great prizes!

- **All you have to do is click** to help Teach for America get $10,000 to ensure that kids in the U.S. get the education they deserve. Click now!

- Treaties are signed and the battles of nations end, but the personal battles of those disabled in war only begin when the guns fall silent. These men and women must struggle to regain health, reshape their lives shattered by disability, learn new trades or professions, and rejoin the civilian world. **At each step, they need help to help themselves.**

- City of Hope is a research and treatment center devoted to battling cancer, diabetes, HIV/AIDS, and other serious diseases. **We seek to turn research ideas into new treatments to bring hope to millions**.

- With one of our biggest matching grants ever, the Salesforce.com Foundation has pledged $500k to College Track in honor of Steve Jobs. College Track helps under-resourced high school students get to college, **and this grant could help 1,200 kids' dreams come true!** Give and get matched today.

- A small nonprofit, OrphanAid Africa, is raising money for their Community Center on Causes, **giving homes to Ghanaian foster children**.

- It's back-to-school time and **unfortunately, lots of kids go to school with empty backpacks**. Help them get the food they need to learn and grow!

- The Flight 93 National Memorial is the only unit of the National Park System that will illustrate the history of September 11, 2001. Approximately 75 percent of the funds necessary to create the 2,200-acre national park have been allocated from public and private sources. **But help is still needed to raise the remaining funds to complete the memorial and provide a place to honor the memory** of the 40 people on board Flight 93 and for future generations to learn what happened on that flight. The Flight 93 National Memorial will be the nation's permanent memorial to the 40 passengers and crew of United Airlines

Flight 93. We're **hoping to raise $11,000** for the memorial during the month of…

- OrphanAid Africa's Foster Family Community (FFC) acts as a temporary shelter for **children removed from situations of abuse**. It serves ill, special needs, or vulnerable children who have no option of extended family care. It is an integrated community where several foster families live in a compound supported by OA.

- Support for a child in the FFC includes their basic needs, such as food, clothing, and shelter. **Twenty-eight children are currently living at the Foster Family Community— 8 are children with disabilities, such as cerebral palsy, who require extra medical attention**. All of these children would benefit significantly with our support!

- On April 27, one of the strongest tornadoes on record destroyed much of the town of Phil Campbell, Alabama. Twenty-eight people died in the storm—including teachers and classmates of the kids at Phil Campbell Elementary School. To add insult to catastrophe, the tornado took their only playground—the TOWN's only playground. The slides were twisted, the swing set, broken. **The kids' best chance to be normal again was gone with the wind**. That's when Kim Sherrill, a local grandmother, reached out to KaBOOM! for help. An Imagination Playground™ is just what these kids need most.

- Help Heaven on Earth Society for Animals and Seth MacFarlane **turn $50,000 into $500,000** and use the funds to build an animal sanctuary.

● Millions of people, most of them innocent children, are at risk in drought-stricken East Africa, at least until the rainy season starts in about 100 days. **Too many children, especially vulnerable to malnutrition and dehydration, have already perished.** Save the Children is already on the ground saving lives. We're rapidly providing food, water, medicine and crucial support to families who have lost their incomes. But we need your support. **Can you and your friends raise $100—that's a dollar a day for 100 days—to help us keep children alive until the rains come?**

● Today, over 5,000 children play on eight love.fútbol soccer fields. Due to your support, those fields not only provide hope for the kids that play on them, but serve as a platform for future development within their communities. We are incredibly excited by our successes, but millions of children without the right to play remain. With the soccer-passionate community behind us, love.fútbol is expanding its operations to Brazil in 2012 and looking forward to continued growth. To prepare for this exciting expansion, love.fútbol is launching the "First Touch" campaign. **Every soccer fan understands the importance of a good first touch—to establish a strong position and move the ball in the right direction. Like any successful endeavor, we need support. And that's where you—the soccer passionate community—come in.**

● The Northern Japan Earthquake Relief Fund was established by the Japanese Cultural and Community Center of Northern California (JCCCNC) to help the victims of the Great Tohoku Earthquake and Tsunami which took place on March 11, 2011. Our relief campaign is a community based and volunteer driven effort. **One hundred percent of the donations received are going directly to citizen relief efforts that are actively on the ground** providing support to the victims through the National YMCAs of Japan and other Non-Governmental Organizations that the JCCCNC has very long relationships with since the 1995 Hanshin-Awaji Earthquake centered in Kobe.

- In the Lower Lempa region of El Salvador, an area plagued by **a cycle of violence** toward women, the Mujeres Ganaderas Cooperative is leading an astounding project. By building a sustainable farming economy this group of women is working to become the breadwinners for their families, which will help them achieve a measure of control over their lives and to **earn a more powerful voice in their communities**.

- Over the past 10 years, Thistle Farms has **grown from a line of two products made by four women in a church kitchen, to a company housed in an 11,000 square foot manufacturing and sales facility that employs 32 women and has a line of over 20 products. Over 100 women have been trained and employed over the past decade**. Our products are available in 140 stores across the country, including a number of Whole Food stores. In celebrating 10 years of Thistle Farming, we are hoping to raise $10,000 during the month of June to provide education and training for 10 new women beginning work—and **a new way of life**—at Thistle Farms.

● Research shows that **90 percent of Americans are aware that child abuse is a serious issue**. Therefore, the Tel-e-thon is designed to engage the public in a dialogue about child abuse prevention, highlighting the many ways everyone can play a role—from getting educated on the issue to advocating for policy change to volunteering for charities that support children and families. Like traditional telethons, ours will offer individuals the opportunity to **make one-time or recurring gifts to Prevent Child Abuse America**. Each hour (with the exception of 12:00 to 6:00 a.m. on April 27) will feature an interview with a special guest or a discussion topic for live chat on our cause. Given the success we have had with social media, and Causes in particular as we now are fortunate to enjoy a following of more than 3.7 million people, the Tel-e-thon provides us with yet one more way to harness the power of social media for even greater impact on our world.

● Our Executive Director has donated his birthday wish to rebuild New Orleans! Please visit this link and click *give* to contribute! **With a donation of $26 in honor of Jim's 26th birthday, you can provide over $750 worth of free labor to families who cannot afford to return to New Orleans otherwise, more than 6 years after Hurricane Katrina.**

● The International Fund for Animal Welfare is offering the top five fundraising individuals the honor of naming a rescued orphaned bear cub at our Bear Rescue Center in

Russia. IFAW's Orphaned Bear Rehabilitation Center cares for **orphaned bear cubs whose mothers have been shot by hunters looking to cash in quick by killing Russian bears**. We need your help to rescue, raise, and release these cubs and to save animals in crisis around the world. **We also need help naming the newly arrived cubs.** Simply donate to this project and then tell your family and friends about this exciting campaign.

2. Send Regular Brief Updates About the Campaign.

Once you create your organization's Causes page on Facebook, it's important to keep current donors and potential donors updated on the activities and successes of your fundraising campaign. The updates that caught my attention the most were those that were limited to one or two sentences and included a link to the organization's website for more detailed information. Even the update bulletins with links to e-newsletters were appealing because of their colorful photographs and clip art to attract a potential donor's eye and get people to read and click through to the campaign's website.

Here are some great brief update examples I've created using the examples from the first section of this chapter.

● Since our campaign began 18 months ago, you and your friends have helped to raise over $40,000. We're only $10,000 from our goal. So close, yet so far.

- Last year, we received $10,000 and met our fundraising goal. It's a new year and we're starting all over again, dollar by dollar.

- To date, your contributions have helped to support 275 disabled veterans returning from Iraq and Afghanistan.

- City of Hope was able to direct 100 percent of your $500,000 in contributions to develop treatments for serious diseases.

- Your contributions have helped the dreams of 1,200 kids come true!

- In the past three months, $25,000 has helped give homes to 200 Ghanaian foster children.

- Thanks! $10,000 came in over the past 30 days. We now have the funding to purchase over 5,000 fruit cups and granola bars for children with empty backpacks.

- With your generosity, we're only 10 percent short of our fundraising goal for the Flight 92 National Memorial.

- Your contributions made it possible for us to provide shelter and safety for 20 new foster families.

- Phil Campbell, Alabama, is five days away from having a KaBOOM! Playground. Thanks!

- Our dollar a day pledges have helped to rescue 1,400 children and reverse the devastating effects of malnutrition and dehydration.

- More kids are experiencing and loving love.fútbol soccer fields thanks to you. In 2012, your contributions to date have opened up 20 new soccer fields!

- Because of your donations, citizen relief efforts have increased by 50 percent.

- Let's have a drum roll! With your support, the Mujeres Ganaderas Cooperative has helped 500 women develop sustainable incomes.

- We are excited to announce that Thistle Farms has extended its June fundraising initiative through September. Please help us meet our goal of $10,000.

- Last night, four million pledges came into our Tel-e-thon. Worn-out volunteers smiled, cried, shouted with joy, and hugged. Your contributions made our event overwhelmingly successful!

- Well, Jim fell short of his birthday fundraising goal; however, it's not too late to make a contribution!

- Thousands of bear cubs become orphaned each year. We're giving you a link to see this pattern of concern and a brief video to show you how we find these bear cubs and what it takes to rescue them once we've nursed them back to health.

CHAPTER 10

Twitter Campaigns

Twitter.com is a popular social media website where more than 100 million persons tweet. Tweets are short posts that are limited to 140 characters (including spaces). Non-profit organizations have turned to Twitter.com to launch their fundraising campaigns. Before you can post your fundraising appeal tweets, you must first make sure you have hundreds (eventually thousands) of followers.

To build your community of followers, first follow others. Look for foundations, corporate grantmakers, actors, sports figures, and high-profile media representatives to follow. If your organization provides food and shelter to the homeless, search for Twitter community members that have the keywords *hunger* and *homeless* in their Twitter profiles. Click on each one and read the full profile. Then click on *Follow*. When you follow others and post messages about your organization and its needs, they will start to follow you to keep abreast of what's happening on your side of the tweets.

In this chapter, I've created tweeting examples to jump-start your Twitter fundraising campaigns.

Elements of Twitter Fundraising

1. Create a Profile Statement for Potential Followers to View.
2. Tweet Your Fundraising Needs.
3. Tweet Buzz and Excitement.
4. Tweet Your Fundraising Progress.

1. Create a Profile Statement for Potential Followers to View

Before you start tweeting, it's important to create a profile for your organization so that other tweeters are able to see *About* your organization and its fundraising purpose. Remember to keep your profile within the Twitter character/space limit (140). If you have to shorten your organization's name to just an acronym, it's okay. As long as you post a link to the organization's website where users can see the full name, mission or purpose, and other characteristics like programs, events, board members, and more, they'll feel confident that they're following a reputable organization.

Here are some awesome perfect phrases profiles I selected from organizations fundraising successfully on Twitter.

- The official Twitter page for Help for Heroes. H4H provide Practical, Direct Support for our wounded, sick & injured. (117 characters with spaces)
- NMEA for Charter Schools was created to allow the diversity in education, talents and resources to be cultivated. (113 characters with spaces)

- We, as the Nourish Team are a partnership of people who care: care for our neighbors and the people around us. (110 characters with spaces)

- SAFE@LAST is a charity working with and on behalf of children and young people at risk through running away. (108 characters with spaces)

- The ACLT charity raises awareness about leukemia and all blood cancers and recruits potential bone marrow donors, blood and organ donors. (137 characters with spaces)

- The motorcycling branch of the Royal British Legion is for anyone with an interest in motorbikes raising money for the Poppy Appeal. (132 characters with spaces)

- Volunteer run nonprofit providing free veterinary care to dogs and cats in Sri Lanka via fixed and mobile clinics. (114 characters with spaces)

- NAPICU is a multi disciplinary clinician lead organisation committed to the development of psychiatric intensive care/low secure services. (138 characters with spaces)

- Mission: We bring to life gospel values of justice, love, compassion, and hope through service, empowerment and advocacy. (121 characters with spaces)

- 14+ women's-only charity aiming to improve mental health/wellbeing, encourage self-development & reduce poverty/economic inequalities. (134 characters with spaces)

- Alleviating poverty through sanitation, water, livelihoods, environment, and empowerment: Wherever the

Need—a great way to spend a penny! (136 characters with spaces)

- We Help Kids Rock!! Our 501(c)3 provides rock school scholarships for kids! (75 characters with spaces)

- Preventing violence against women and girls through education and art. (70 characters with spaces)

- It's All for the Kids! A Boston-based non-profit; support of many local athletes including Tim Wakefield, Jason Varitek, and Jerod Mayo! (136 characters with spaces)

- Project Foundation is a nonprofit 501(c)(3) working to build strong foundations for a better future around the World. (117 characters with spaces)

- Bringing HIT to the Safety Net Providers in the Carolinas. (58 characters with spaces)

- Children of Promise, NYC (CPNYC) is a community based, non-profit organization, working with children who have incarcerated parents. (132 characters with spaces)

- Project BOSS is Bringing Out Successful Sisters, a match program designed to connect professional women with mentoring programs for youth. (138 characters with spaces)

- One Life to LIVE and a Whole World to Build…Let's Move !!! (63 characters with spaces)

- Haiti1Stop is a one-stop informational site for individuals and organizations working towards rebuilding Haiti & creating self-sufficiency. (139 characters with spaces)

2. Tweet Your Fundraising Needs

Remember, keep your tweets to the 140 character or less limit if you want them to be accepted by twitter.com. The shorter the tweet, the quicker you'll grab the attention of followers. Once you have their attention, tweet your fundraising needs. On Twitter, it's important to use a lot of shortcuts for standard English words. Numbers are written numerically versus being spelled out; *and* is typed as *&*.

Here are some example fundraising needs tweets I created that incorporate perfect phrases and build on the organizations profiled in the first section of this chapter.

- It takes $5K in resources to help 1 wounded, sick, & injured hero. Click here to donate. (87 characters with spaces)

- We need your help 2 develop diversity education software. Please help us change charter school education modules! (113 characters with spaces)

- Help us nourish 100 new children in Kentucky mining towns. $50 grows a field of vegetables. When harvested, 200 children are fed. (129 characters with spaces)

- 28,000 kids under age 16 ran away last year! Some will die; others will be victimized in horrible ways. Help us keep them safe! (127 characters with spaces)

- 4,000+ bone marrow donors are needed nationwide. Thousands of people are dying because of the short donor list! Need $1K for outreach. (134 characters with spaces)

- Poppy fields are needed by drug companies, food manufacturers, & millions of bees. Help our poppy fields! $500 U.S. plants a field. (131 characters with spaces)

- Unneutered and unvaccinated pet & street dogs interact daily; creates transmission of diseases & creation of unwanted pregnancies. (130 characters with spaces)

- Your $ are needed to replenish funds used to care for psychiatric patients. (75 characters with spaces)

- The victims we serve need advocacy. Our funds are nearly gone. Please help! (75 characters with spaces)

- Derby women face daily *inequality* and *poverty*. *Without funding, they will never realize* their potential. Please donate! (119 characters with spaces)

- A penny an hour can make a difference! Save a life! Please see our videos of clients that are dying. (100 characters with spaces)

- Children, ages 7 to 17 years old, need the character development skills acquired at a Rock School. Donate today! (112 characters with spaces)

- Last year, 476 women were brutalized by their partners. Their recovery is long. Art helps! We need your $! (106 characters with spaces)

- Today's kids don't have a chance without mentors, positive parents, and a caring community. We make a difference with your $! (125 characters with spaces)

- Our world is at risk! Help us make an appeal to the World Congress of Nations. Legal and appearance will cost $100k+. (117 characters with spaces)

- HIT is on the brink of technology disaster. New emerging innovations are needed. Please help! (93 characters with spaces)

- 250,000 children have 1 or more parents in jail or prison. For them, kinship care is not working. Please help us step up our advocacy! (134 characters with spaces)

- Mentor recruitment takes time and $. $1,500 gives us the resources to recruit new mentors. Can you help? (104 characters with spaces)

- Make a difference in the life of one youth and you might be surprised at the outcome. Please buy 10 tickets for our fundraising dinner. (135 characters with spaces)

- Haiti is no longer on the news. No one is writing checks or flying over to help. Will you? (90 characters with spaces)

3. Tweet Buzz and Excitement

By buzz and excitement, I mean that you must keep your Twitter followers tuned in to (reading) your tweets. Buzz and excitement can be about special events, a large donation, moving your offices from cramped quarters to larger ones, or anything else that is happening at your organization.

Here are some example buzz and excitement tweets I created that incorporate perfect phrases and build on the organizations profiled in the earlier sections of this chapter.

- Lots of excitement here about this weekend. Retired General Bullwinkle will be the guest speaker for the Board meeting! (119 characters with spaces)

- Weekly Buzz: Our diversity software module received two awards from the American Education Diversity Council! (109 characters with spaces)

- Yahoo! An out-of-state landowner donated 200 tillable acres to our cause! (73 characters with spaces)

- SAFE@LAST won $10,000 worth of free advertising from the Metro Advertising Council! (83 characters with spaces)

- We are excited! International film star that had a hush-hush bone marrow transplant & is thriving will lead our educational outreach drive! (139 characters with spaces)

- Just signed a contract with Seeds for Life to sponsor 100 new poppy fields! (75 characters with spaces)

- United Kingdom Veterinary's Association has agreed to be advocates for our cause! (81 characters with spaces)

- Moving to a new facility this year! Will have therapeutic gardens and recreational areas. Wow! (94 characters with spaces)

- Our new spokesperson is Amy Grant. We're over the top with excitement! (70 characters with spaces)

- At last night's graduation, 130 Derby women graduated! Starting a new life with new skills and paychecks soon! (110 characters with spaces)

- Our next mission begins in 30 days. Volunteers are so excited to be digging 1,000 new wells and taking over 10,000 immunization kits. (130 characters with spaces)

- Last night's Rock School performance at the White House left everyone on cloud nine! (84 characters with spaces)

- The grand opening for the new Healing Gallery is tonight! Ribbon cutting at 7 p.m. Come on over! (96 characters with spaces)

- Next year, we're opening 10 new hockey rinks in Massachusetts! (62 characters with spaces)

- Our appeal to the World Congress of Nations resulted in new legislation for improved world air quality! (103 characters with spaces)

- We're all abuzz! Free Webinar with Dr. Bev Browning on Grants for HIT projects. Open to anyone. First come, first register! (123 characters with spaces)

- 50 of our kids' parents will exit prison in 12 months. New transitioning parent project will teach parenting skills before their release! (137 characters with spaces)

- 400 new mentors in orientation! 400 young girls are waiting and ready! (70 characters with spaces)

- Witness a nation of youth making a difference in Detroit, Michigan, every day! Tune in to CNN on December 24 and see us move! (123 characters with spaces)

- What's the buzz? 20 commercial planes will carry over volunteers, food staples, tents, cots, lumber, and more! (110 characters with spaces)

4. Tweet Your Fundraising Progress

If you're going to go after donors on Twitter, it's critical that you let them know how their contributions are making a difference. When your organization is falling short of its fundraising goal, it's time to put the call out for more $ via your tweets. When those dollars are coming in, tweet updates on your progress. Finally, when you reach your fundraising goal, remember to post a tweet to thank your followers.

Here are some example fundraising progress tweets I created that incorporate perfect phrases and build on the organizations profiled in the earlier sections of this chapter.

- Can't believe how far we've come! You've helped us to meet 60 percent of our annual fundraising goal! (100 characters with spaces)

- $50,000 in 50 days! We couldn't have done this without your contributions and retweets to potential donors! (107 characters with spaces)

- 1,500 new trees were planted in a burned-out forest. Only 4,500 more trees to go before the next decade. (104 characters with spaces)

- $150,000 raised at our black tie event. 10 corporate sponsors (found on Twitter) gave the most ($75,000)! (105 characters with spaces)

- With your help, we've registered 500 new bone marrow donors! (60 characters with spaces)

- Year-to-date, you've helped us reach 50% of our annual fundraising goal! (72 characters with spaces)

- Raised $10,000 in one day at SuperMart near the Greyhound Race Track! Goal 4 next week is $15,000 @ Dogs R Us! (110 characters with spaces)

- 4,072 counseling hours sponsored with your help! (48 characters with spaces)

- 24 victim advocacy groups and growing! Your $24,000 made this happen! (69 characters with spaces)

- Only $20,000 short of our capital campaign goal for new offices and classrooms! (79 characters with spaces)

- We asked you for $1,000 to drill a well and you gave $100,000. Over the moon and into the valleys for Central America! (118 characters with spaces)

- Passed the plate (or hat) at last night's Rock School performance and collected $2,000 for new musical instruments! (115 characters with spaces)

- Collection jars @ gallery & around town are filling up! Looks like we'll meet our fundraising goal of $10,000 for new art supplies soon! (136 characters with spaces)

- Weldon Hockey Rink fundraiser was a huge success. Over $7,000 raised from two local churches! (93 characters with spaces)

- New legislation passed resulted in worldwide awareness. Donations are pouring in. Over $400,000 and counting! (109 characters with spaces)

- HIT has hit the jackpot! Thanks to tweeters, we raised $40,000 in 7 days! (73 characters with spaces)

- Governor heard about our Twitter fundraising efforts and added $100,000 to the next fiscal year's budget for correctional parenting program! (140 characters with spaces)

- The Dollar Bill Foundation audited our program last month. Found results that led to them offering us $50,000 for next year! (124 characters with spaces)

- Sold 1,000 tickets; raised $100,000! Thank you notes going out today! (69 characters with spaces)

- Hit ground running and building in Haiti! Camera crews everywhere caught our frenzy of activity. Media helps us raise $100,000 in 24 hrs! (137 characters with spaces)

PART III

PERFECT PHRASES FOR TELEPHONE AND FACE-TO-FACE CAMPAIGNS

CHAPTER 11

Telephone Campaigns

B efore the Internet, the only way to solicit funds from potential donors (prospects) was either through a face-to-face meeting, mail via the postal service, or by telephoning the person in hopes of making a personal connection with your best appeal voice. While a telephone call may seem easy, if you're not prepared, the call can result in a hang-up or listener disengagement fast.

In this chapter, I will share perfect phrases for executing successful telephone campaigns.

Elements of Telephone Campaigns

1. Catch the Listener's Attention with *A* to *Z* Words That Resonate.

2. Follow Basic Verbal Content Delivery Rules.

3. Create a Flexible and Natural Script.

1. Catch the Listener's Attention with A to Z Words That Resonate

First, research the organization and individual you're approaching for funding and know their frequent phrases, buzzwords, and personality. How can you do this? Use the Internet to search for the organization's website. Conduct a second search using the contact person's name (first and last) + city + state. For example: If you're searching for John Bronson and you know that he lives or works in Concord, Massachusetts, you would type: John Bronson + Concord, MA.

The search engine will find all website addresses with any of the two words John and Bronson in the title or content plus Concord, MA. There might be 400,000 John Bronsons on the Internet, but this search will locate all incidences of John Bronson and Concord, MA on the same link. This type of search allows you to find John Bronson's social media profiles, any newspaper articles that mention his name, and all other occurrences of John Bronson and Concord, MA. Adding the plus sign eliminates all of the nonrelevant listings of John Bronson and narrows the search results down to the John Bronson that you want to speak with in Concord, MA. Also, search for videos or audio files with speeches or media interviews so you can listen to John's voice, speech patterns, and for words that are repeated or emphasized. Take copious notes to help you hone your ability to know when you're either reeling John in as a funder or losing John with a tacky or boring telephone script.

Between John's website and other electronic media, make an A to Z list of words that you want to use in your telephone fundraising campaign. It's likely that you won't have time to incorporate all of the buzzwords (jargon and action words) that you compile; however, even selecting five of common connection words will extend the time that a listener will listen to your voice appeal for funding.

Here's an example of my *A* to *Z* word list for creating perfect phrases for telephone fundraising campaign scripts:

● Awesome *A* words that activate a giving mind frame:

Accelerate	Adapt	Arrange
Accomplish	Address	Articulate
Achieve	Align	Assess
Acquire	Allocate	Assist
Act	Anticipate	Attract

● Believable words that begin with *B*:

Balance	Boost	Budget
Bargain	Bought	Build
Begin	Brief	Built
Bolster	Broaden	

● Captivating words that begin with *C*:

Calculate	Charge	Communicate
Capable	Check	Compare
Capture	Clarify	Compile
Catalog	Coach	Complete
Categorize	Collaborate	Compose
Cause	Commence	Conceptualize
Chair	Commitment	Conclude

Condense	Connect	Convey
Conduct	Conserve	Cooperate
Confer	Consider	Coordinate
Confidence	Contact	Create
Confirm	Contribute	Cultivate

● Distinguishing words that begin with *D*:

Decide	Describe	Discuss
Decrease	Detect	Dispatch
Dedicate	Determine	Distinguish
Deduce	Develop	Distribute
Define	Devote	Diversify
Deliver	Differentiate	Document
Demonstrate	Direct	Draft
Depreciated	Disclose	Duty
Derive	Discover	

● Engaging words that begin with *E*:

Earn	Enable	Enlist
Effect	Encourage	Enrich
Elect	Engage	Ensure
Eliminate	Enhance	Expand
Emphasize	Enlarge	Expedite
Employ	Enlighten	

● Fantastic words that begin with *F*:

Facilitate	Forecast	Fund
Familiarize	Fortify	Fundraising
Finalize	Forward	Further
Focus	Foster	

● Guiding words that begin with *G*:

Gather	Govern	Guide
Gauge	Grade	
Generate	Grant	

● Humbling words that begin with *H*:

Handle	Hence	Host
Head	Highlight	Humanitarian
Heavy	Hitting	
Help	Horizon	

● Illuminating words that begin with *I*:

Identify	Initiate	Interact
Illustrate	Innovate	Interpret
Impart	Inspire	Introduce
Implement	Install	Invent
Improve	Institute	Inventory
Incorporate	Instruct	Involve
Increase	Insure	

● Jaw-dropping words that begin with *J*:

Jeopardize	Judging	Juggle
Join	Judicious	Justify

● Kaleidoscopic words that begin with *K*:

Keen	Keystone	Knee-deep
Keeping	Kindle	
Key	Knack	

● Levitating words that begin with *L*:

Label	Lead	Liquidate
Labor of love	Learn	Locate
Landing	Legacy	Log
Launch	Lighten	

● Mesmerizing words that begin with *M*:

Maintain	Measure	Model
Manage	Mentor	Moderate
Map	Merge	Modernize
Market	Minimize	Modify
Master	Mission	Monitor
Maximize	Mobilize	Motivate

● Noble words that start with *N*:

Navigate	Noteworthy	Novelty
Negotiate	Notify	Nuance
Nominal	Not with-	Nurture
Nonstop	standing	

● Obligatory words that start with *O*:

Observe	Orchestrate	Outline
Obtain	Order	Outstanding
Offset	Organize	Overhaul
Operational	Orient	Oversee

● Persuasive words that start with *P*:

Package	Perceive	Philanthropist
Participate	Perform	Pilot

Pioneer

Plan

Prepare

Present

Preserve

Prevent

Prioritize

Process

Produce

Program

Project

Promote

Propose

Provide

● Quotable words that start with *Q*:

Qualify

Quality

Quantify

Quid pro quo

Quintessential

Quota

● Resonating words that start with *R*:

Raise

Rank

Reason

Recall

Recognize

Recommend

Rectify

Reduce

Relate

Render

Renew

Reorganize

Repair

Replace

Represent

Research

Reserve

Resolve

Respond

Restore

Restrict

Retain

Retrieve

Revitalize

Route

● Sizzling words that start with *S*:

Sample

Schedule

Scrutinize

Secure

Select

Share

Simplify

Solve

Spearhead

Specialize

Sponsor

Stakeholder

Stimulate

Strategize

Streamline

Strengthen

Structure

Substantiate

Suggest

Summarize

Supervise

Support

Sustain

● Telling words that start with *T*:

Tabulate	Thankful	Tithe
Tackle	Tightrope	Tour
Tailor	Time	Track
Target	Timeframe	Trailblazing
Teamwork	Timeline	Transform
Territory	Time permit-	Transmit
Tether	ting	Traumatic

● Unveiling words that start with *U*:

Uncover	Untimely	Upgrade
Understand	Unusual	Upheld
Undertake	Unveil	Use
Unify	Update	Utilize

● Validating words that start with *V*:

Value	View	Visualize
Vanguard	Vision	Voice
Verify	Visit	Volunteer

● Winning words that start with *W*:

Weigh	Window	Worldwide
Widen	Wish	Worth
Will	Witness	Write

Note: Typically, words starting with X are not commonplace in any type of fundraising campaigns.

● Yes-producing words that start with *Y*:

Yearly	Yoke	Your
Yearn	You	
Yield	Young	

● Zeroing in words that start with *Z*:

Zeal	Zest	Zone
Zenith	Zigzagging	

2. Follow Basic Verbal Content Delivery Rules

I have incorporated the action and buzzwords from the first section of this chapter into telephone scripts of perfect phrases for telephone fundraising campaigns. While some of these terms may seem a little far-fetched, remember, depending on your prospect's vocabulary, website verbiage, cultural nuances, and colloquialisms, the usage of these words may be commonplace. Using a commonplace approach that is prescriptive to each prospect will yield a higher contribution rate compared to writing one script to fit all and having 99 hang-ups out of 100 telephone calls.

● Rule 1: Research, write, and practice your script (record yourself and then play it back so you know where you sound canned or robotic).

- Rule 2: Keep your script short; respect the potential donor's time.

- Rule 3: Greet the donor by name. Sound happy to meet and/or speak with him or her.

- Rule 4: Introduce yourself (by name, job title, and organization).

- Rule 5: Tell the donor why you are calling. In other words, why is this telephone campaign needed? What are you trying to raise funds for? Why? What is the urgency?

- Rule 6: Be prepared to answer questions without hesitation. Always tell the truth and stick to the script for the facts. Do not embellish your organization's situation or need.

- Rule 7: Ask for the donation. Remember to ask for a specific amount. Don't waiver and don't shift the tone of your voice from confirming to doubtful! Be prepared to tell donors how they can remit their donation. You can send them a prestamped envelope, or you can direct them to a donation website for your organization.

- Rule 8: Get a commitment date for the donation so you can note when to follow up with the donor.

- Rule 9: Confirm the donation amount (some prospect researchers refer to this as the asking twice rule) and incoming date.

- Rule 10: Thank the donor for his or her time and donation. End on a positive note with one sentence and wait for donors to bring the call to a close on their end.

Note: Follow the three minutes maximum rule for all words coming out of your mouth and off of your script.

3. Create a Flexible and Natural Script

After you've researched your prospective donors and you are ready to talk to them using their own frequently used words and phrases (examples are bolded below), you're ready to write your customized script for each donor. You can use an outline like the one I've presented in Rules 1 through 10 in the previous section of this chapter.

Here are some telephone fundraising campaign scripts that incorporate words from section 1 and follow the outline in section 2:

● Hi, Father Marquette! This is Dillon Lawrence, Volunteer Student Yearbook Leader at Noblesville High School! I'm calling to ask you to help our school raise the needed funds to publish this year's Book of Memories for Noblesville High School. I know you read the headlines last week; the Board of Education has cut $500,000 from the high school's budget. We're in a dilemma. By the way, did you know that 50 percent of our graduating class attended St. Theresa's School through eighth grade before transferring over to our school? Father, you and your team really prepared an **outstanding** group of **accelerated** and **accomplished achievers**! A full-page advertisement is only $250. Yes, or course, you can review the ad copy. We need your check by the 30th of this month. The Yearbook Committee has set up a web page on the school's website where you can donate using a credit card or e-check. Will this work for you? I'm taking notes on today's conversation. Can I **confirm** that you're buying a $250 full-page advertisement? You'll be submitting the $250 via our web page? I can e-mail your ad copy to? Oh yes, it's fathermarquette@StTheresa.org, correct? Father, we appreciate your sponsorship! The Committee is **thankful** for your time and commitment to **contribute**! We're reserving a complimentary copy of the new yearbook for you, and someone will deliver it as soon as they're back from the printer. **Peace be with you**, Father Marquette!

● Hi Mavis! This is Carol Meriwether, Capital Campaign Chair at Flint Osteopathic Hospital! I'm calling on behalf our Donor's Forum to invite you to become a **sponsored** member of the Donor's Table. Yes, Carol, you're correct; the Donor's Table is a group of 12 women **philanthropists** who each commit to raising or directly donating $100,000 annually toward the hospital's housing fund for interning medical school students. If you'll remember, Jessica Long, one of our longtime Table members, died suddenly three months ago. Yes, it was sad for everyone that knew Jessica. Carol, we urgently need you to fill this position! You have so many connections via your various alumni groups and statewide associations. We believe that $100,000 a year will be an easy goal for you, and we have **confidence** that you're one of the few women **capable** of reaching—and even exceeding—this amount. We're all really excited! I'd like to invite you to a **commitment** tea next Thursday at 3 p.m. at Jane Sorkin's house. Of course, her address is 1334 Giving Lane. It's an informal and informational meeting where you can ask questions, we ask you questions, and of course, you can make an early contribution toward your $100K goal; the last three incoming members gave $10,000 each. Can I let the committee know that you'll be there? I'd be glad to pick you up and take you back home if that's okay. Of course, I know your address. You live next door to my sister-in-law, Lois McGraw. I know, it's a small world! Let me **confirm**, you're available to come; I'm picking you up, and you may be bringing an early donation check of at least $10K. No problem, our Treasurer will be there and can give you a receipt on the spot. Thanks, Carole. I'm so excited; see you next week! My mobile number is 555-555-5555 if you need to reach me before Thursday.

● Hi, Patrick! This is Jenny Lawson, Director of the Mid Delta Resettlement Fund in Lawson, Mississippi! I only need a few minute your time today. I've been looking at our donation's history, and I see that you contributed to the Fund annually for five years. However, for the past three years, we lost your **valued support**. Last year, we resettled 100 new families from third world countries to the Delta region. The face of Mississippi is changing faster than dollars are being allocated for living needs! Patrick, I heard your last speech at the Civic Club. Your love for Mississippi and your **legacy** as a **philanthropist** is what makes you such a **valued** friend. We can't **accomplish** our **mission** without your **support**. Your theme of **connect**, **discover**,

collaborate, and **enable** resonated in my mind long after your speech. We need you back! Can I count on you for a $5,000 **commitment** this year? Great! I can come by your office to drop off a contribution receipt and pick up your gift on Friday. What time is convenient for you? I'm so honored and excited to have you back in the Fund's family! I'll have the receipt typed up for $5K, correct?

● Hi, Connie! It's Mack Davison, Capital Campaign Manager at the Southwest Center for Justice! I'd like to arrange a time when I can come by and drop off a campaign packet. First, did you read about our efforts to **raise funds** to **boost** our legal fund? We're **cultivating** new community **stakeholders** that **value** the Center's **model** for immigration justice. I know that your bank supported the Acculturation Awareness Initiative two years ago, so I feel like the time is right to sit down and talk about how you can help us with the campaign. We're looking for a $100,000 investment pledged over two years. I believe that is the maximum amount of a direct grant from the CRA funds, correct? I know that your board meets at the end of the month. Can I come by today and leave a packet? Thanks, Connie, I knew we could count on you to **assist** the Center!

CHAPTER 12

Board of Directors Campaigns

In board of directors fundraising campaigns, two levels of campaigning are needed. The first level of successful solicitation is to know how to use perfect phrases to speak to your board members about their own contributions to your organization. I'm not talking about the time they commit as volunteer board members. I'm talking about the need for them to contribute financially on an annual basis to your organization. Remember, when you are out in the community asking others for contributions, it's important to be able to state that 100 percent of your board of directors members have made a financial commitment to your organization. The board must believe in what your organization does first before others will believe that their contributions will make a difference or impact. The second level of successful solicitation is to train your board members to help with all types of fundraising efforts including capital campaigns.

In this chapter, I'll cover the dialogue you'll need to practice in order to get your board of directors moving from just attending meetings to actually helping bring in contributions to your organization.

Elements of Board of Directors Campaigns

1. Dialogue to Encourage Your Board Members to Give at a 100 Percent Level.

2. Fundraising Scripts for Board Members to Use When Soliciting Contributions in the Community.

1. Dialogue to Encourage Your Board Members to Give at a 100 Percent Level

Any type of fundraising requires an internal effort first. On a personal level, you would not ask strangers for money before first going to your family members. On a professional level, you can't call, mail, or knock on the doors of prospects until you have a 100 percent commitment from your board of directors. This can often be a touchy subject, and most executive directors don't want the job of talking to the board about giving financial contributions. The antiquated way of thinking is that because the board comes to regular meetings and participates at the committee level, that's all they need to give. Wrong! Grant makers and individual donors want to see an internal commitment first before they consider giving to your organization. Now, for the nitty-gritty! It will typically be the development director that makes the presentation to the board of directors about board responsibilities.

Here are some resource links to help you prepare for this presentation. These links talk about exactly what constitutes boardsmanship:

- Society of Nonprofit Organizations—www.snpo.org/samples/V180613.pdf

- Tony Poderis—http://www.raise-funds.com/1998/annual-fund-giving-getting-guidelines-for-trustees/

Here are some sample perfect phrases for fundraising dialogues you can fine-tune and practice when educating your organization's executive director and when soliciting the board of directors for their own contributions to your organization:

- **Conversation with Your Executive Director About Board Giving Responsibilities**

   Hi, Mary. Can I talk to you about how the community will scrutinize our organization when we launch this capital campaign? Thanks, I appreciate your time and I'll be brief. In my last Association of Fundraising Professionals meeting, our guest speaker was the board president of the Spokane Community Foundation. He spoke about board member accountability and how grant-making agencies and individual contributors expect an organization's full board of directors to demonstrate financial support first before any outsiders are approached for grants or contributions. Apparently, the Washington Foundation Association has been educating and encouraging their member foundations to require evidence of internal financial support in the form of board member contributions. In addition, even our local United Way requires that its board give fully at some level of affordability first before going out into the community to solicit support for its capital campaign. I think we need to get on the bandwagon too! Mary, our next board meeting is in three weeks. Can we add contributor expectations to the agenda? Do you want to approach the board, or would you like for me to compile some statistics and examples of board member accountability trends and present this idea of the board giving first. We can even refer to this as the Board First Initiative. What do you think?

● **Direct Appeal to Your Board of Directors**

Hi, everyone. I've asked for time on the board's agenda to share the feedback that I'm getting from potential funders and contributors. As you know, we have been calling and meeting with potential donors throughout the community. When I start to talk to them about the new animal shelter and what it's going to cost along with how *we* need their help financially, the first question that I'm being asked is, "Has 100 percent of your board contributed to this cause?" Of course, I could tell a lie, but then that would not reflect well on our organization. So, I'm here today to ask each of you to consider pledging an annual contribution amount to the East New Hampshire Animal Rescue Shelter. I know that you give your time, talent, and more on a regular basis through volunteerism. However, outsiders can't see this or even fathom how we can ask the community to give when our board is not giving first. Remember, the amount you pledge does not have to be grandiose or impose a financial hardship. I've spoken to some fundraisers at smaller grassroots nonprofits in the community, county, and throughout the state. Their boards have always or recently started making financial contributions to their organizations. These contributions can be as small as $100 annually. If they can do this, I believe that *we* can do this too! I'm open for ideas on how to get started, and I'm ready to answer any questions that you might have about how to do this anonymously so no one board member has to feel bad about a lower contribution than another member.

- **Conversation with an Irate Board Member Who Thinks Just Showing Up at a Meeting Is Enough**
  - ❖ Your Board Member: Jim, I sat through your presentation and grew hotter by the minute! I can't believe that you expect me to pull out *my* checkbook and make a contribution to this organization! I agreed to be on this board and to serve a three-year term. For me, giving my time is a sacrifice because I'm away from my job and family. It takes me one hour to read and understand the board agenda, old meeting minutes, and any other documentation that arrives at the last minute each month! It's a 30-minute drive to and from your facility from my home or work. I sit in an uncomfortable chair listening to committee report after committee report drag on and on! I also sit on four subcommittees! I'm a practicing attorney,

and I'm giving you thousands of dollars of my time! Don't we value our thrift store volunteers using some national hourly rate to show their in-kind contribution to us? Why can't you apply that hourly rate formula from independentsector.org to my time and just write down that I give X amount of dollars annually?

❖ Your Perfect Phrases Response: As just a staff person, I truly appreciate everything that you and the other board members do to lead this organization toward financial success. The current sitting board is the best board we've ever had. Remember, I've been here 20 years, and I've seen the good, the bad, and the ugly. With this board, I've watched and learned from the *great*! I appreciate everything, Marty! Our entire staff knows the high value and skill sets that each board member brings to this organization. However, when I step out into the community to ask for contributions, they don't see the value of your volunteer work with our organization. Instead, foundation program officers and individuals with substantial giving abilities are asking brutally hard questions that I can't truthfully answer and still get a grant or contribution. They are asking me, "How many of your board members donate money to your organization on an annual basis?" They do not ask how much each of you personally donates; however, they are asking if 100 percent of the board writes a contribution check annually. The perception is if the board isn't fully giving money—even a check as small as $100—why should an outsider want to invest in our organization. Marty, can you see my dilemma? If I lie, that reflects on the organization. Anyone can request a list of our contributors since we're a public charitable organization. If I tell the truth, we've lost a potential grant or contribution. How would you feel if I arranged for you to meet with some potential donors and a few of the local foundations so that you can explain why our board members are not contributing some level of money on an annual basis?

Note: Remember, you can fine-tune these conversations to fit your organization and the situation at hand. In some instances, it may be wise to take this conversation to the board's executive committee first (top elected officers) before presenting this to the full board of directors.

2. Fundraising Scripts for Board Members to Use When Soliciting Contributions in the Community

Rule 1 of Boardsmanship 101: Each board member will learn how to solicit contributions for your organization. Remember, each board member is your link to identifying and approaching new donors, from individuals to corporate and foundation grant makers. It's important that you or someone else (don't overlook an outside organizational capacity building trainer) prepare the board for soliciting contributions from individuals and connecting directly with potential foundation and corporate donors.

Here are some perfect phrases for board members to use when soliciting contributions:

- ## A Conversation Following a Game of Golf with Three Potential Donors

  Hey guys, let's get some refreshments before we get back on the road. While we're winding down, there's something I'd like to talk to the three of you about. It's pretty serious, and I think you might have some solutions. You know that I've been on the board of directors for the City of Harmony for nearly a year now, and I'm impressed with what we're doing for this community. Our staff and outreach workers have walked the streets and talked to gang members first-hand about the escalation of violence in our city. They've risked their lives at times to push everyone, including the gangs, toward a harmonious community. Our largest community partner is the local police department—and well, I think you've read the headlines on the budget cuts for every city department. We've talked about hiring some laid-off police officers to team with our staff when they are walking the streets and counseling gang members. We want our staff and volunteers to be safe. However, we're in a major financial dilemma. This was not a planned budget expense, so we're forced to look outside of the organization for contributions. Of course, staff is applying for grants aggressively, but it's not enough! We need $100,000 in less than three months or there won't be any more harmony on our streets! Mark, you manage the trust department at the bank? Can you review your trusts to see if there is a way to grant some of the monies to our organization? Steve, in your position as the manager of Shop Rite, you can probably recommend charities to your corporate headquarters that they'll support, right? Just tell me what you need from our staff, and I'll help get a funding request to you as quickly as humanly possible. Alex, I know that you retired five years ago and you're enjoying this type of leisure. Is there any way you can look at your finances and consider making a direct contribution to the City of Harmony? Everything contributed is tax deductible. We're in a bad place and just need a hand up in handling this dire situation. When is a good time to follow up with each of you? I'd like to give you some packets with our mission, annual report, additional financials, the project budget for using laid-off police officers, and a copy of our Internal Revenue Service letter of nonprofit determination for your files.

● A Conversation with a Member of Your Church

Hi, Jill. I really look forward to seeing you in church every week. Your family always seems so happy and full of love and life. I've really tried to keep myself busy since Jim died. Did you know that I volunteered to be on the board of directors for Little Souls Foundation? Yes, we collect new shoes for infants and toddlers and donate them to shelters for the homeless. We also help organizations that serve children with special needs like leg braces or orthopedic shoes. Donations have been declining for the past two years. I guess a child without shoes doesn't really matter to someone who's never been a parent! My children, even though they all live in other states, all came home to help me when Jim died. I never appreciated being a parent more than when they all filled the house with concerns, love, and ideas on how to memorialize Jim in our community. Anyway, Jill, enough about me! I am in charge of finding new donors for the Little Souls Foundation. I'd like to invite you to a board meeting to hear more about our mission and our struggles before you make a decision about being a regular contributor. Would you like to attend our meeting next month? It will be a perfect time to meet our full board and administrative staff. Also, I can give you a contributions packet with additional information on ways to give. I'm so excited that you'll be able to attend. I'll e-mail you with the location, directions, and time. Jill, I just want to thank you in advance for considering helping the homeless children in our community.

● A Conversation with a Neighbor

Hey, Jerry, do you have a few minutes to meet at the fence line? Wow, your grass always looks so well manicured. I see you working in the yard every day. The whole neighborhood shines because of your landscaping and yard maintenance skills! I'm on the board for the Apache Junction Zoological Society. We're responsible for managing the zoo and making sure that the financial needs for our programs and projects are met through grants and contributions. Recently, I accepted the chair position for our fundraising committee. Jerry, can you remember taking your kids to the zoo when they were small? Oh yes, don't we all still take our grandkids when they can find the time for us? Jerry, I think you can help the zoo as well as give yourself a new tax write-off before the end of the year! I want to give you this brochure that our committee created for potential donors. We have three levels of sponsorships. The Cub level is for donors who can contribute up to $500 annually. The Care Bear level is for donors that can give more than $500 up to $1,000. The Golden Bear level is for major donors that contribute over $1,000. Each level comes with increasing benefits and recognitions. Jerry, would you consider making a contribution before the end of the year? What additional information do you need in order to make a decision? Thanks for your time, Jerry. I'm excited that you're going to be helping me find money and possibly other potential donors for the zoo! I know that you've belonged to the 100 Club for years. Again thanks, Jerry!

- **A Conversation with the Board Member's Employer and the Human Resources Director**

Jenny, did you know that most employers in this community have employee matching gift programs? I checked our human resources manual, but I didn't see any reference to our employee matching gift program. Do we have one? Have you ever considered creating a program where if an employee contributes X amount of dollars to a local charity, the company will match the contribution with a 25 percent, 50 percent, or 100 percent contribution to the charity. Of course, I think it should be limited to charities where employees volunteer. After all, our efforts in the community extend the company's goodwill and presence, too! I'd like to be on a company committee to create a matching gift program. What's my interest? I have been on the board of directors for the Austin State University Foundation for three years. We are always looking for ways to open our doors for corporate responsibility programs. Many corporations allocate 5 percent of their annual profits toward charitable community reinvestment. A matching gift program encourages employees to do community service, join boards, and give a portion of their earnings to tax-exempt charitable organizations. How can we get started?

● **A Conversation with a Foundation Program Officer**

Carl, thank you for taking the time to meet with me today! I know that your schedule is busy, and I'm sure you get many requests for meetings like this. My entire board thanks you! I'm here on behalf of the board of directors for the Sickle-Cell Anemia Research Institute. Here's an information packet for you to review when you get a chance. We've been around since 1968, and we got started with an endowment fund established by the founding board of directors. When the economy was soaring, the interested earned on the endowment (by the way, the Nonprofit Research Foundations Group manages our funds) was phenomenal. However, lately, with this declining economy, the interest has been minimal. This has impacted our general operating expenses and has caused us to hold back on aggressive research for a cure. Carl, someone told me that a member of your family was diagnosed with sickle-cell anemia, is that true? Well then, you must know what it means to conduct aggressive research to find a cure. We're looking for new donors, and I think that your foundation is a perfect match! I've done my research, and I know that you fund endowments. How can we get your partnership in helping to boost our endowment fund? What is the next step? Of course, I can arrange a meeting between our full board and your endowment staff. Let's touch base with some dates, times, and places tomorrow, okay? I'm so excited, Carl!

CHAPTER 13

One-on-One Fundraising Meeting Campaigns

A ll fundraisers find themselves scheduling and sitting in dozens of one-on-one meetings with potential individual donors. Development officers and prospect researchers use highly polished appeal scripts to bait, reel in, and catch new donors daily. What's the secret? None! It's about articulating your message and talking about your organization's needs so much that it no longer sounds like a script.

In this chapter, I will give you some short scripts for telling your organization's needs and selling the idea of getting funds from previous and potential donors.

Elements of One-on-One Fundraising Meeting Campaigns

1. Telling Your Organization's Needs.
2. Selling Stakeholder Investment to Potential Donors.

1. Telling Your Organization's Needs

Before you can ask potential donors for money, it's important to set the stage for asking or selling by telling them about your organization's needs. These needs can range from project seed money to general operating funds. Talk to your executive director and board members to determine what they have prioritized as the organization's most urgent needs and the individual line item cost of each item or project in need of funding.

You can approach individuals with specific needs (one-time) or continuing needs (planting annual donor seeds).

Here are some perfect phrases to tell about your organization's needs:

● Hi, Leslie, thanks for taking the time to meet with me today! Last year, Floating Hope performed 546 surgeries on refugee children that were flown to the United States by faith-based sponsors. The donations covered the cost of their round-trip coach transportation from their home countries to Los Angeles; one escort ticket (volunteer or parent or other caregiver), and lodging for the escort during the child's hospitalization. Physicians donated their time and skills to perform the surgeries free of charge. While it sounds like everything is covered financially, it's not. The supplies, medications, and hospital equipment needed to round out Floating Hope must all be purchased in bulk on a weekly basis. Equipment breaks or becomes outdated quickly. Last year alone, these costs exceeded $5 million. Even if we had a special event every month, there is no way we can raise $5 million without identifying new donors.

● Hi, Mr. Mickelson, it's a pleasure to finally meet you in person. I know we've talked a lot, but this is a real honor! I only need about 30 minutes of your time today. I'm here on behalf of the board of directors for Shiloh Valley Hospice. We're a 501(c)(3) nonprofit organization that was founded in 2000. Since then, we've grown from serving 10 terminally ill patients a year to caring for 250 patients' year-to-date. The average physician-referred patient is in our care anywhere from 30 days to 120 days. While 70 percent of our revenues come from third-party healthcare providers, 30 percent comes from individual contributions. Lately, the number of individual donors has been declining and we're in a major financial crunch!

● Hi, Frankie, greetings from our executive director, who apologizes for not being able to make this meeting! I think she told you that little Sally had her tonsils out this morning and she's at the hospital with her all day today. Well, I won't take up too much of your time today, but I do have an important need to discuss with you. The Diocese has released its budget for the next fiscal year, and it's not looking too good for social services agencies like ours. For years, the Bishop allocated $200,000 a year toward our general operating expenses. In less than three months, that amount drops to *zero*! We're all sweating bullets! Frankie, we're not worried about our jobs; we're worried about cutting back on the services we offer and having to put high-risk clients on a waiting list. Our only answer for this crisis is to reach out to the community for help.

● Hi, Judge Garth, it's an honor to meet you! Please thank Julie for setting up this appointment so quickly. I'll get to the point. Halfway Home, our aftercare residential facility, lost part of its roof with the last hurricane. While insurance covered the repair, the three days of rain didn't help. Our temporary tarp cover collapsed and water poured into our sleeping quarters and commercial kitchen. I guess you've probably already guessed that we do not have a building fund to replace furnishings or appliances. These kids (the ones you refer to us) have no place else to go. They are not ready to go home yet. We've created an emergency fund to get this mess cleaned up and get our kids off of the floor and back into their bunks. The kitchen is operating out of coolers and boxes, and it's hard to prepare a decent meal on a hot plate connected to a 40-foot extension cord running to the business next door. Judge Garth, I asking you for a direct donation to help us out of this crisis. I'm also asking that you talk with your colleagues about help-ing us out.

● Hi, Libby, thanks for meeting with me today on such a short notice! I'll be brief. The fire department's brush truck died yesterday. The truck was purchased in 1985 and has been repaired at least 100 times. Pancake breakfasts, bake sales, and the annual carnival proceeds have been the source of the repair funds. Yesterday, the truck's engine block cracked, and it's being retired to the scrap metal yard. The brush truck handled extreme off-road terrain. We thought it was unstoppable...but yesterday it was stopped permanently. Libby, you know how much we need a brush truck. You saw the fire that we fought on Miracle Mountain last year. It took everything we had plus help from neighboring fire departments. A cloud of depression has set over the fire department, and the mayor's pulling what hair he has left out. There is no money for a new brush truck!

2. Selling Stakeholder Investment to Potential Donors

People must feel connected to your organization before they will become contributors. You have to show them the connection by knowing a few tidbits about them before you meet with them. Researching prospects is an art. Knowing your potential donors 360 degrees (both their work and personal lives) leads to higher selling rates. Use the Internet, ask around town, and even talk to other individuals in your community that know each potential donor.

Remember, when you're ready to close the sale, you can ask for cash at the meeting or a future pledge. You can also create a wish list and give it to them to see the cost of each wish and decide what they want to give to fulfill the wish.

Here are some selling perfect phrases to make the invitation and close the deal:

- Leslie, I'm inviting you to become a new stakeholder in Floating Hope. I know that before you decided to become a pharmacist and start your own 56-store chain, you attended medical school. You remember what it was like to witness medical miracles in the making. Today, on behalf of our Board of Directors, I'm inviting you to become a Floating Hope stakeholder. What does this mean? It means that you are willing to become an annual contributor by helping Floating Hope serve more children and save more lives. Can I count on you, Leslie? This year, we need 100 new donors that can give $5,000 each. You'll be a founding contributor of our new Floating Hope 100 Club! What a surprise, Leslie. I did not expect a check today. I'm overwhelmed!

- Mr. Mickelson, may I call you Jack? I'd like to invite you to make a financial investment in Shiloh Valley Hospice. I just remembered, I think you're already familiar with our services. Wasn't Marge Jackson your wife's sister? One of our staff remembers you and your wife coming to see Marge while she was in hospice care. We did everything we could for Marge to make her last few weeks as comfortable as possible. Dying is sad but unavoidable . . . Jack, can you be one of our Gold level donors? Being a Gold level donor means that you would be willing to pledge $20,000 yearly toward uncovered expenses at Shiloh Valley Hospice. You would have until the end of the year to write the check, but I would need to have a signed pledge form today for our records. I can't tell you how much this means to our board, staff, volunteers, and patients, Jack. Uh, Jack, did you make a mistake? Your pledge card says $50,000. Is that correct? I'm speechless!

● Frankie, I heard that you were a parish administrator for 10 years in another town in the Diocese. Is that correct? So you know the Bishop? What a small world! Frankie, we're having a $10K fundraising dinner in two months. There will be ten $1,000 seats at each table of donors and 50 total tables. Can I put you down for filling one donor table? You can personally purchase the 10 seats or find 9 other donors to share your table with. I brought your packet of tickets to expedite your work in filling your table. Frankie, on behalf of our Board of Directors, I want to extend a warm welcome to the Frisco Center Social Services family! Here's your information packet with fliers, letters, and a CD with templates for approaching other donors. Your generosity will mean a lot to our clients! Please let me know if you need additional ticket packets. Thanks again for your time, Frankie!

● Judge Garth, I read your biography when you presented at the County Bar Association's meeting a few months ago. I did not know that you were an orphan raised in the foster care system. I was surprised to know that you spent a year in the county correctional facility as a juvenile. To admit that gives encouragement to others that are struggling. Judge Garth, I brought you some information packets to share with your colleagues. Can we count on a check from you soon? What can I do to facilitate this process for you and your colleagues? Of course, I'd be glad to come to your chambers on Thursday night. You'll have how many colleagues there for the presentation? 20? I'm so excited! What time shall I arrive, sir? I truly appreciate your time today and the time you're opening up on Thursday evening for me to make this appeal to your colleagues!

● Libby, wasn't your grandfather a fireman at our station? What a small world! Libby, I brought you the manufacturer's specifications and the cost sheet for the new brush truck. It's going to run around $60,000. Libby, I know you need time to think about this; however, I'd like to tell our board members that you're going to help us. Can we count on you for a donation? I'm overwhelmed, Libby! You want to donate half of the $60,000 needed? Words cannot convey our appreciation and surprise!

CHAPTER 14

Service Club and Civic Organization Campaigns

In every community across the country, there are service clubs or civic organizations that award grants and give contributions for local charitable, educational, and scientific causes. While some of these groups have formal grant applications, many merely require a fundraising appeal presentation. Typically, these oral presentations are made by one person to the entire service club or civic organization group at one of their meetings.

A sampling of service clubs and civic organizations includes:

- Civitan International
- Elks of the United States
- Jaycees
- Key Club International
- Kiwanis International

- Lions Clubs International
- Masonic Clubs
- Rotary International Foundation
- Shriners of North America

In this final chapter, I'll give you a sample script outline and then a full script of perfect phrases to guide you when making these types of presentations.

Elements of Service Club and Civic Organization Campaigns

1. Fundraising Appeal Presentation Outline.
2. Sample Fundraising Appeal Presentation Script.

1. Fundraising Appeal Presentation Outline

This is the suggested outline for an oral fundraising appeal presentation to members of service clubs and civic organizations. Remember to contact the club to find out when and where they meet, the average number of members in attendance, and the maximum length of presentation time that you'll be allotted. Check to see how many handouts (copies of your presentation) you'll need to bring. Ask if there will be time for questions and answers.

Here is the outline for oral presentations:

- Give your name, title, and organization.
- List the communities served by your organization.

- Give your organization's annual budget (last year and current year).

- Tell the amount you are asking for from the club or organization.

- List any organizations that have already given funds for this project.

- Tell if the requested funds will be applied to a new project, expansion project, general operating support, or specific program expenses.

- Share the mission of your organization.

- Briefly describe your project and/or the purpose for which funds are being requested, including your intended results.

- Describe the target population to be served (number, age, group, and other characteristics).

- Tell how your organization will evaluate the success of the project if funded.

- Indicate if this is your first time asking for funds from the group.

- If any members of the group volunteer with your organization, mention this.

- Mention that you're including a copy of your IRS tax-exempt letter, organization budget, project or program budget, and list of board members with your handout.

- Call for questions.

- Thank the group for their time.

2. Sample Fundraising Appeal Presentation Script

I've given you the outline for preparing your fundraising appeal presentation. Now it's time to give you a perfect phrases script example. Remember, there may be time constraints on your presentation, so trim section content where needed to quickly deliver your information and still leave time for questions from group members.

Here is an example of how to roll out this script to club or organization members:

- Hi, I'm Dr. Beverly Browning (Dr. Bev or just Bev), founder and director of the Grant Writing Training Foundation.

- The Foundation services communities across the United States including 38 cities in Maricopa County, the service region for this club.

- Last year's annual budget was $146,000; this year, $150,000.

- On behalf of my board of directors, I am seeking $6,000 from this club.

- We previously received a $10,000 grant from the U.S. Bancorp Foundation.

- The $6,000 requested from your club will support specific program expenses related to Nonprofit Board of Directors Boot Camp training for Maricopa County grassroots to midsize nonprofit organizations.

- The mission of the Grant Writing Training Foundation is to provide affordable grant-related and nonprofit capacity-building training programs to educate, enable, and empower charitable, educational, and scientific nonprofit organizations.

● The one and one-half day training program consists of Boardsmanship 101 skill sets and organizational, leadership, and resource development. Board members and senior staff leave with increased understanding of how to build the board's capacity; increased awareness of the organization's strengths, weaknesses, opportunities, and threats; ability to create and execute a one-year strategic plan with benchmarks; and fundraising skills.

● The target population for the Nonprofit Board of Directors Boot Camp is grassroots to midsize nonprofit organizations in Maricopa County. Most of the organizations that are candidates for attending have newly formed boards or established boards whose board members are not fulfilling their board responsibilities. The board is the foundation for every organization. A weak board results in a failed organization.

● A pre-and-post survey is administered at every Boot Camp to determine the percent of new knowledge gained from the training. In addition, six months after the Boot Camp, each attending organization will be contacted to follow up on the results and impact of the new knowledge learned in training.

● This is the first request for funding from your club.

● Two club members have previously attended a Nonprofit Board of Directors Boot Camp; six members have attended a two-day Grant Writing Boot Camp.

- I have handouts for everyone that provide the information shared in my presentation. In addition, I've attached our IRS letter of nonprofit determination, the current budget for the Foundation, and how the $6,000 will be used. Our board of directors roster is last in the packet.

- Do you have any questions?

- Thank you for your time and consideration for supporting the Grant Writing Training Foundation.

The Right Phrase for Every

Perfect Phrases for Building Strong Teams

Perfect Phrases for Business Letters

Perfect Phrases for Business Proposals and Business Plans

Perfect Phrases for Business School Acceptance

Perfect Phrases for College Application Essays

Perfect Phrases for Communicating Change

Perfect Phrases for Conflict Resolution

Perfect Phrases for Cover Letters

Perfect Phrases for Creativity and Innovation

Perfect Phrases for Customer Service, 2e

Perfect Phrases for Dealing with Difficult People

Perfect Phrases for Dealing with Difficult Situations at Work

Perfect Phrases for Documenting Employee Performance Problems

Perfect Phrases for Employee Development Plans

Perfect Phrases for ESL Everyday Business

Perfect Phrases for Executive Presentations

Perfect Phrases for Fundraising

Perfect Phrases for Health Professionals

Perfect Phrases for Icebreakers

Perfect Phrases for Landlords and Property Managers

Perfect Phrases for Law School Acceptance

Perfect Phrases for Lead Generation

Perfect Phrases for Leadership Development

Perfect Phrases for Lean Six Sigma

Perfect Phrases for Letters of Recommendation

Perfect Phrases for Managers and Supervisors, 2e

Perfect Phrases for Managing Your Small Business

Perfect Phrases for Medical School Acceptance

Perfect Phrases for Meetings

Perfect Phrases for Motivating and Rewarding Employees, 2e

Perfect Phrases for Negotiating Salary & Job Offers

Perfect Phrases for New Employee Orientation and Onboarding